An Introduction to
Programming in Prolog

D1551579

Patrick Saint-Dizier

An Introduction to Programming in Prolog

Translated by Sharon J. Hamilton

Springer-Verlag
New York Heidelberg Berlin
London Paris Tokyo Hong Kong

Patrick Saint-Dizier
LSI Université Paul Sabatier
Toulouse, France

This work is a translation of the French volume *Introduction to Programming in Prolog* by
Patrick Saint-Dizier, published by Eyerolles - Paris.

Library of Congress Cataloging-in-Publication Data

Saint-Dizier, Patrick, 1954-
    [Initiation à la programmation en Prolog. English]
    An introduction to programming in Prolog / by Patrick Saint-Dizier.
    p. cm.
    Translation of: Initiation à la programmation en Prolog.
    Includes bibliographical references.
    ISBN 0-387-97144-0 (alk. paper)
    1. Prolog (Computer program language) I. Title.
QA76.73.P76S25   1989
005.13'3—dc20   89-39409

Printed on acid-free paper.

Camera-ready text prepared by the author.
Printed and bound by R.R. Donnelley & Sons, Harrisonburg, Virginia.
Printed in the United States of America.

9 8 7 6 5 4 3 2 1

ISBN 0-387- 97144-0 Springer-Verlag New York Berlin Heidelberg
ISBN 3-540- 97144-0 Springer-Verlag Berlin Heidelberg New York

Preface to the English Edition

This book is an introduction to Prolog (<u>Pro</u>gramming in <u>Log</u>ic). It presents the basic foundations of Prolog and basic and fundamental programming methods. This book is written for programmers familiar with other programming languages, as well as for novices in computer science, willing to have an original introduction to programming. The approach adopted in this book is thus based on methodological elements together with some pragmatic aspects.

The book is composed of two parts. In the first part the major aspects of programming in Prolog are presented step by step. Each new aspect is illustrated by short examples and exercises. The second part is composed of more developed examples, which are often games, that illustrate major aspects of artificial intelligence. More advanced books are given in the bibliography and will allow the reader to deepen his or her knowledge of Prolog. Prolog was first designed in France at G.I.A., Marseille, with a specific syntax. We have adopted here a more common notation, defined at Edinburgh, which tends to be an implicit norm.

At the end of each chapter of the first part, there are exercises that the reader is invited to do and to test on his or her machine. Complete answers are given in Appendix A, at the end of the book. It is necessary to do these exercises several times, looking at answers, till they become straightforward. These exercises are relatively neutral with respect to a particular application domain; they constitute, in fact, a set of tools useful in many applications.

The reader is asked to consider Prolog as a specialized language designed for symbolic deduction. It is not adapted to classical management or scientific computations, although applications can be programmed using Prolog. Prolog is a powerful tool for developing artificial intelligence applications.

This book is the synthesis of several years of experience in teaching Prolog and logic to novices, undergraduates, and graduate students. I would like to thank the colleagues with whom I exchanged many ideas, P. Fresnais and B. Houssais, and also several students who have helped improve my teaching of Prolog by numerous insightful questions. I also thank Janis Horne and Sharon Hamilton for their fine English translation of the original French text. Finally, I am indebted to my wife Edith, who proofread the text and suggested modifications and clarifications, and who was responsible for the formatting and typesetting of the book.

                                    P. Saint-Dizier

Contents

Chapter 1

Representing Facts in Prolog

Programming in Prolog consists essentially of three activities:

(1) declaring facts,
(2) stating deduction rules based on these facts,
(3) asking questions.

These activities are introduced in the first three chapters of this book.

In this first chapter, after introducing the concept of a *tree*, we show, through everyday examples, how one can introduce knowledge into a Prolog system by defining facts. This chapter is at the same time an introduction to the most elementary concepts of Prolog and an introduction to classical logic, also called first-order logic.

1. Trees

We begin our presentation of the elementary syntax of Prolog by defining a fundamental data structure: *the tree*. Trees are the basis of all the processing done in and by Prolog.

Every tree has a single *root*, which is shown above the rest of the tree in diagrams like the one following. From the root emanate a finite number of *branches*, which lead to *nodes*. The nodes can subdivide again into branches and nodes. The position of the branches in a tree is fixed and cannot be modified without changing the tree. Finally, the nodes at the bottom of the tree at the end of each branch are called *leaves*.

In a tree, the branches serve simply to establish dominance or sibling relationships between the nodes and the leaves. Here is a tree:

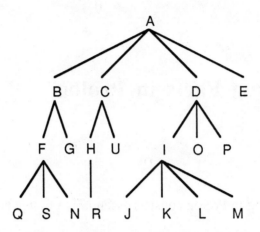

In this tree the nodes have been labeled. The root is labeled **A**, the nodes are **B, C, D, F, H, I**, and the leaves are labeled **Q, S, N, G, R, U, J, K, L, M, O, P**, and **E**. Note that the branches vary in length and that any number of branches can emanate from a node. The technical term branch does not distinguish between a single elementary branch (e.g., **A----> B**) and a series of elementary branches (e.g., **A----> B----> F----> Q**).

A tree allows the definition of family relationships: these can be expressed concretely in terms of family trees. In the preceding examples node **B** is said to be the *parent* of F and G. Conversely, **I, O**, and **P** are said to be the *children* of **D**. Finally, **F** and **G** are *siblings* because they have the same immediate *father*.

The *depth* of a tree is the maximum number of successive elementary branches between the root and a leaf. The depth of the tree in the preceding example is 3, because from the root to the leaf **Q**, for example, there are three elementary branches:

     A----> B
     B----> F
     F----> Q

A *subtree* of a tree consists of any node of the tree, along with all of that node's descendants. The resultant subtree has the node as its root and is itself a tree. Note that a tree can be reduced to a single element, for example, **P**. Here, for example, is a subtree of the tree in the preceding example:

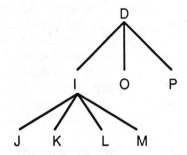

In this subtree the root is **D**. **I** is the sole node, and **J, K, L, M, O,** and **P** are the leaves.

The tree is the only data structure used in Prolog. For notational convenience, trees are represented in a "flattened" fashion with the aid of parentheses. The siblings in the trees are separated by commas, while a parent-child relationship is expressed by introducing parentheses. For example, the subtree given above is represented in this way as

D (I (J,K,L,M), O, P)

and the initial tree as

A(B(F(Q,S,N),G),C(H(R),U),D(I(J,K,L,M),O,P),E).

It is essential, however, to keep in mind the initial tree structure because it clarifies the underlying mechanism of the Prolog system.

2. Facts

Prolog essentially consists of an automatic proof mechanism and several predefined functions. This mechanism permits effective reasoning based on the knowledge that the programmer brings to the system.

We now show how to introduce knowledge into the Prolog system, knowledge that Prolog can then use to answer queries. This knowledge is represented as either *facts* or *rules*. In this chapter we show how to define facts. Rules are discussed in Chapter 3.

The statement *Tom speaks to Luke* can be broken down into

two "objects," identified by the names Tom and Luke, and into a relation that can be designated *speak to*. In logic, the names Tom and Luke are considered to be *constants*. It is then possible to define a structure that establishes a relationship between Tom, Luke, and the act of speaking. In logic, this structure is called a *predicate*. A predicate is composed of a *name* (here, **speak_to**) and any number of *arguments*, including none. A predicate has a truth value, which is, in the simplest case, either true or false. We then obtain

speak_to(first argument,second argument)

and we take it as a convention that the first argument represents the speaker, while the second argument represents the listener. This convention is arbitrary, but must be strictly adhered to once defined. The statement above is represented by a fact in Prolog and is written

speak_to(tom,luke).

Note that, for the purposes of uniformity, capital letters have been omitted. Moreover, there are no spaces between the different parts of a relation name or within an argument. The spaces must be either removed or replaced by a special character, most frequently _, which increases the readability of the words, as in **speak_to**. Words are also often standardized. Here, for example, *speaks* is in the infinite form. Finally, a fact is always terminated with a period.

A programming language traditionally consists of two complementary levels:

(1) A *syntactic level*, which describes the form of the different entities of the language. There is a name associated with each type of entity. The statement **speak_to(tom,luke).** is called a *term*.

(2) A *semantic level*, which assigns a meaning to each type of syntactic entity. The statement **speak_to(tom,luke).** is called a *fact*.

In comparison with classical programming languages, a fact corresponds approximately to a data item.

A term can be represented by a tree. The above example is represented as

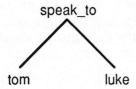

Facts may have any number of arguments, but once defined, a relation like **speak_to** always has the same number of arguments, and each argument always has the same meaning. Note, however, that Prolog exercises no a priori control over the contents of the arguments. It is therefore the responsibility of the programmer to verify the accuracy and coherence of the data.

Here are more examples of facts:

John is the brother of Mary.
becomes: **is_brother_of(john,mary).**

Catherine has Paul for a brother.
becomes: **has_brother(catherine,paul).**

Edith is blonde.
becomes: **blonde(edith).**

Max gives Rover to Martine.
becomes: **give_to(max,rover,martine).**

The predicate **has_brother(,)** is called a *two-place* predicate because it takes two arguments. The predicate **blonde( )** is a *one-place* predicate, and the predicate **give_to(, ,)** is a *three-place* predicate. **Blonde** and **give_to** are represented in the form of trees as follows:

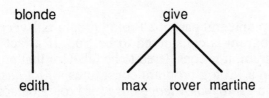

3. Properties and Relations

It is important to understand the meaning of a Prolog fact

(**has_brother, blonde, give_to**, etc.): It states a *property* of an object or a general relation among objects. The arguments of a fact are the concrete values that identify the entities satisfying this property or relation. Thus, the predicate

give_to(max,rover,martine).

consists of a general relation *give* with three arguments, denoting, respectively, the giver, the given entity, and the recipient. Max, Rover, and Martine are then three concrete entities that make the predicate **give_to** true: *Max gives Rover to Martine.*

It is possible to define a fact without arguments, as, for example, **nice_weather.** This fact has an absolute character; it cannot receive different entities as arguments.

When a fact has a single argument, it usually states a property of a group of objects that it allows as arguments. This makes it possible to characterize a set of objects that have a certain property:

blonde(edith).
blonde(john).
blonde(harvey).

In this example, it is stated that the members of the set

E = {edith,john,harvey}

have the property of being blonde.

A fact represents a *relation* when it has at least two arguments. A group of facts that describe a particular property or relation corresponds to a group of tuples, instances of a relation in a relational database.

Facts are an integral part of a Prolog program. Every fact that belongs to a program is considered to be true. If a fact does not belong to a program, it is considered to be false for that program. A group of facts in a Prolog program constitutes a *fact base*. A fact base is a part of a Prolog *knowledge base* (or Prolog database). The term "knowledge base" is not unique to Prolog; it is used in artificial intelligence to indicate a collection of structured knowledge from which inferences may be drawn.

In a Prolog program facts are independent of each other. They may be about anything; Prolog does not test for coherence or cohesion among them. Moreover, as we shall see in more detail in the following chapters, the order in which the facts are stated in the program is not important.

4. Introducing Facts in Prolog

There are essentially two ways to create a fact in a Prolog system:

(1) by using an editor to create a fact, which is then interpreted by Prolog;
(2) by interactively "asserting" facts into the Prolog system.

When it is desirable to save a group of facts for several executions, it is most convenient to create a file (or several files) that contains a set of database facts. This file is then interpreted by the Prolog system in response to the command

[filename].

where **filename** is the name of the file.
For example, if the file is called **base1**, the instruction is:

[base1].

If there are several files to interpret, they can be given in a list, as in the following example:

[file1,file2,file3].

The predicate **assert** is used to add a new fact during the course of an execution without using a file; **assert** is predefined in the system and is used as shown below:

assert(fact).

To add the fact

is_brother_of(andrew,julie).

the following command is used:

assert(is_brother_of(andrew,julie)).

The fact is then automatically included in the Prolog program.

The call

[user].

allows the user to play the role of the input file. **CTRL-D** is used to finish entering the program.

We shall return to the method of adding facts in Prolog in the chapter devoted to databases. Complete examples of Prolog executions are given at the beginning of the following chapter.

Exercises

The solutions to these exercises, as well as comments on them, are given at the end of this book.

Ex. 1.1

Consider the following tree:

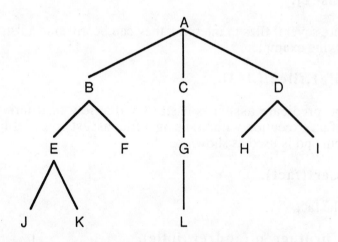

(a) What is the name of the root of this tree?
(b) What are the names of the nodes?
(c) What is the depth of this tree?
(d) List the parent of **B**, the children of **D** and **C**.

(e) Give the subtrees with roots **B**, **E**, and **L**.
(f) Put these subtrees in parenthetical form.

Ex. 1.2

Represent the following statements as Prolog facts:

(a) Jack gave Fido to Julie.
(b) Jack is the brother of Julie.
(c) John is courageous.
(d) It is raining.
(e) John is reading Hamlet.
(f) Shakespeare is the author of Hamlet.
(g) Shakespeare is the author of Romeo and Juliet.
(h) Mozart is the composer of the Magic Flute.

Chapter 2

Querying the Fact Base

After stating facts and creating a fact base, we can question (or query) the system about the knowledge we have given it.

1. Elementary Questions

An *elementary question* has the same syntax as a fact. To distinguish it from a fact, it is preceded by a minus sign: - . This minus sign may be provided automatically by the system; it is preceded by a question mark: ? . Strictly speaking, a question is composed of the signs ?- followed by *goal*.

Thus, the question:

Is Paul the brother of Catherine?

is written:

    ?- is_brother_of(paul,catherine).

This, in turn, asks at the program level:

Does a fact exist that states that Paul is the brother of Catherine?

Prolog then searches through the fact base to see if such information has been previously entered. If it has, the Prolog system produces the response true (or yes). If no such information has been entered, the response false (or no) is produced.

If the response is true, we say that the fact

    is_brother_of(paul,catherine).

matches (or unifies with) the question:

   ?- is_brother_of(paul,catherine).

because

   (1) the name of the relation is exactly the same in the fact and
   the question, and
   (2) the corresponding arguments are identical.

We now construct a more complete example to enable us to
continue our explanations. We use the following fact base:

   is_brother_of(paul,catherine).
   is_brother_of(paul,lucy).
   is_brother_of(john,luke).
   is_brother_of(luke,michael).
   is_brother_of(michael,edith).
   is_brother_of(paul,martine).

The order in which facts are declared does not affect the truth
value of the results, since Prolog traverses the fact base until the
answer is found. Notice also that, when a constant (e.g., Paul)
appears several times, it always designates the same individual.

We now question Prolog about this small fact base. To
answer the question:

   ?- is_brother_of(michael,edith).

the system examines each of the facts in the order in which they
have been declared. When it finds a fact that matches the question,
it responds true. However, the system does not stop; it continues
to traverse the fact base right to the end. If the desired fact is found
several times, the system will produce the response true as many
times as it is found. It is an interesting peculiarity of Prolog that it
finds all the possible solutions to a problem, particularly when the
problem is complex and may be solved in several ways. There are
methods of stopping the search as soon as a fact that answers the
question is found. These methods are explored in Chapter 8, when
we address the problem of control.

   If we now turn to the logical view of Prolog, the set of facts
given to the system can be seen as a set of axioms (the data that are
considered a priori to be true). A question is then a theorem, which
one attempts to prove from these axioms. Prolog is the mechanism
that allows the system to construct a proof and, consequently, to
say wether the question is indeed a theorem deducible from the
axioms (answer yes) or not (answer no). Prolog's proof

mechanism begins with the question; this is why the question is also called a *goal*. Finally, note that, if the question

   ?- q(---).

cannot be proved, this does not necessarily mean that **q** is false, but simply that there does not exist a fact **q** in the fact base that matches the question.

2. Questions with Variables

When we ask the question:

Whose brother is Paul?

we mean that we would like to know all the values of **X** for which Paul is the brother of **X** or, in other words, that **is_brother_of(paul,X).** is true. This question is written in the following manner in Prolog:

   ?- is_brother_of(paul,X).

To differentiate a variable (here **X**) from a constant, the convention in the majority of versions of Prolog is to begin the names of variables with a capital letter. All names of constants begin with a lower case letter. In certain other versions of Prolog the symbol ∗ precedes all variable names.

The concept of variable in Prolog is slightly different from that used in classical programming languages. In Prolog, a variable represents a specific entity, whereas in a classical programming language, a variable is a convenient method of designating a place in the computer's memory. This difference will be better understood once we have explained how a question is evaluated in Prolog.

The response to the above question **is_brother_of** is not unique: in the fact base, Paul is the brother of Catherine, Lucy, and Martine. We now examine how the set of values **X** for which the query is true is determined by Prolog.

At the beginning of the evaluation of the above question, **X** is not bound to any value. That is, **X** is free. The task of the Prolog system is to find in the fact base all the possible values that can be bound to **X** to answer the question. To find all the values of **X** that make the question **is_brother_of(paul,X).** true, Prolog proceeds as follows (for this first explanation, we do not deal with the implementation details of Prolog itself):

(0) Consider the first occurrence of the fact **is_brother_of** in the fact base. We call the fact currently being considered by the system the *current fact*.

(1) Scan all occurrences of **is_brother_of** in the fact base, starting from the current fact, until there is found a fact that unifies with the constants that appear in the question (in the example above, **is_brother_of** and **paul**).

(2) Bind **X** to the value that is found in the corresponding argument in the fact. This fact becomes the current fact.

(3) Return (print) the result.

(4) "Unbind" **X**. **X** is now free to be bound to another value.

(5) As long as the system has not scanned all the occurrences of the fact **is_brother_of** in the fact base, proceed to the next fact and return to step (1). Otherwise, the evaluation is finished.

The variables that appear in a Prolog question are said to be existentially quantified.

This means that **is_brother_of(paul,X).** is true if there exists a value for **X** such that **is_brother_of(paul,<this value>)** is true. Prolog goes beyond finding a single such **X**; it provides all the possible instances of **X**.

When there are several solutions to a question, such as in the example above, the first answer found is the one returned first. The next answer is obtained by typing the character **;** , followed by a carriage return. In the example above we would have

X = catherine;
X = lucy;
X = martine;
yes

To end the enumeration, simply type a carriage return.

To write out the result in cases in which the result is not written out automatically, it is necessary to introduce a writing command. We can print the contents of a variable by adding, after the question, the predicate

write(X).

This predicate prints the contents of **X**. The predicate **write** is predefined in the system as a reserved word, which the user cannot redefine. The question and the **write** predicate are now separated by a comma, and the period that previously terminated the question in Prolog is now placed after the writing command

?- is_brother_of(paul,X), write(X).

The question now reads: Find **X** that satisfies the predicate **is_brother_of(paul,X)** AND print the contents of **X**. **X** is unbound from its value only after the answer is printed. We discuss this point in a more general fashion in the following section.

3. Conjunction of Elementary Questions

We might wish to ask a more complex question, such as

Do Catherine and Lucy have Paul for a brother?

This question means, at the Prolog level: Does there exist a fact that states that Paul is the brother of Catherine AND is there another fact which states that Paul is the brother of Lucy? It is expressed in Prolog in the following manner:

?- is_brother_of(paul,catherine),
is_brother_of(paul,lucy).

Prolog will reply true (or yes) to this question if and only if both facts exist in the fact base, which is indeed the case here. The comma that separates the two facts is equivalent to a logical AND.

To answer this question, Prolog first checks wether the first fact is true. If not, it responds false (or no). If it establishes that the first fact is true, Prolog then tries to prove the second fact. If the second fact is also true, then the answer to the question is true (or yes), and false otherwise.

We now consider a more complex question, one that contains a variable (in general, a question can contain as many variables as we like):

Do Catherine and Martine have a common brother?

To express this problem in Prolog, we reason in the following manner:

(1) Let **X** represent a brother of Catherine, if one exists.
(2) The answer to the question is then true if there is also a fact that states that **X** is the brother of Martine.

This is expressed in Prolog as

**?- is_brother_of(X,catherine),
is_brother_of(X,martine).**

The variable **X** is used twice in the question to designate the same individual.

The Prolog system first attempts to answer the first part of the question: find an **X** who is the brother of Catherine. If it finds such a value (e.g., Paul), then the second occurrence of **X** in the question is immediately and automatically bound to this value:

**?- is_brother_of(paul,catherine),
is_brother_of(paul,martine).**

Next, the system searches the fact base to see wether there exists a fact that matches the second part of the question, which no longer contains a free variable. Since answering the first part of the question had the effect of binding **X** to Paul, it is now necessary to show that **is_brother_of(paul,martine)** is true. If such a fact exists, the question has a solution. A question is then true if and only if there exists a solution that satisfies each elementary part of the question.

With regard to Prolog's execution mechanism, if Prolog finds that the value to which **X** is bound in the first part of the question does not satisfy the second part of the question, it reconsiders this value by freeing **X** in the first part of the question and searching for a new solution that will satisfy the entire question. If such a solution is not found, the response to the question is false.

The act of reconsidering a previous choice is called *backtracking*. Backtracking is implemented in the Prolog system by means of a system of stacks. The user does not have to be concerned with this backtracking mechanism and can instead state his or her knowledge in a declarative fashion without having to consider the execution mechanism. Note that, if there are several possible answers to a question, Prolog also backtracks so that it finds all of them.

The phenomenon of backtracking can be illustrated with a brief example. Let us consider the following fact base, which is composed of facts of the form **know(X,Y)**, where **X** knows **Y** without this relation necessarily being reciprocal:

    know(john,luke).
    know(edith,colette).
    know(ronald,colette).
    know(hagar_the_horrible,snoopy).
    know(edith,hagar_the_horrible).
    know(ronald,archie).
    know(hagar_the_horrible,archie).
    know(edith,archie).

The question

Which people are known by both Edith and Ronald?

is expressed in Prolog as

    ?- know(edith,X), know(ronald,X).

At the level of Prolog's resolution system, the question to be proved can be represented by a small tree diagram, where each branch designates a sub problem:

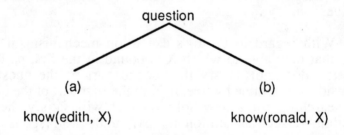

Here we have two sub problems, (a) and (b). Prolog always starts looking for the solution with the sub problem on the far left in the tree, here (a). The complete resolution process is shown below:

(1)
(a): **X** is bound to **colette**.
(b): The value of **X** is automatically carried over to the
   second part of the question:

know(ronald,colette) is true, so the first answer is **colette**.

The solution can be shown schematically as a tree:

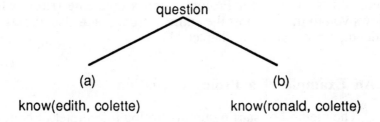

(2) **X** is unbound from **colette** and the search continues.
(a): **X** is bound to **hagar_the_horrible**.
(b): Prolog cannot find a fact to prove:

know(ronald,hagar_the horrible).

The second attempt at a proof therefore fails.

(3) **X** is again unbound from its value. The search continues:
(a): **X** is bound to **archie**.
(b): Prolog finds a fact to prove:

know(ronald,archie).

We now have a second solution: **archie**.

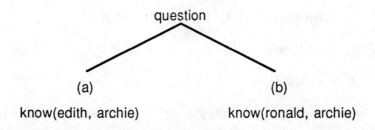

(4) **X** is unbound, but there is no other value for part (a) of
the question.

The search terminates after the fact base has been completely traversed.

The example presented here is extremely simple; we shall be looking at some more complex ones in the following chapters. A simple method of following what happens during a Prolog execution is to use your Prolog system's predicate **trace**, which allows you to trace almost the entire search; **trace** also allows you to debug a program (see Chapter 11).

4. An Example of a Prolog Execution

The method of starting up the Prolog interpreter or compiler may differ appreciably in different versions of Prolog. The usual way is to type

prolog

without a terminating period. An introductory banner then appears, followed by the prompt

?-

You may then load in your file of Prolog facts, called, for example, base1:

?- [base1].

As soon as Prolog finishes interpreting this command, it waits for a question from the user. You may then ask questions about your fact base. Consider the last example given in this chapter:

?- know(edith,X), know(ronald,X).

Prolog responds with

X = colette

If you type a carriage return, Prolog responds **yes** and waits for a new question. If you want another solution to the question, type a semicolon followed by a carriage return, immediately following the first result:

X = colette;

and Prolog gives the following correct response:

X = archie

To leave the Prolog environment, type

?- halt.

Slight differences exist among the different versions of Prolog. These are minor and are often clearly mentioned in the user manuals. Certain versions of Prolog give all the responses to a question at one time. This may be convenient when there are only a few correct responses but may also cause a flood of responses, particularly when debugging a program!

Exercises

Ex. 2.1

Write the following questions in Prolog:

(a) Who are the children of Catherine? (use **child_of(X,Y)**, where **X** is a child of **Y**).
(b) Is Edith blonde?
(c) Are Paul and Martine the children of John?

Ex. 2.2

Assume the relation **taller_than(X,Y)** where **X** is taller than **Y**, and the following fact base:

```
taller_than(john,luke).
taller_than(john,marie).
taller_than(martine,marie).
taller_than(catherine,john).
taller_than(mark,john).
taller_than(mark,martine).
```

What does Prolog respond to the following questions?

(a) ?- taller_than(X,john).
(b) ?- taller_than(X,Y).
(c) ?- taller_than(mark,X).
(d) ?- taller_than(catherine,Y), taller_than(Y,Z).

Chapter 3

Expressing Rules

Prolog rules are an extremely powerful means of expression allowing us to express knowledge in a more general way.

1. Advantages of Rules

We now consider an example to introduce the concept of a rule. Consider the relation

child_of(X,Y).

which states in a general fashion that **X** is the child of **Y**, and the following knowledge base:

child_of(john,jack).
child_of(catherine,marcel).
child_of(edith,sylvia).
child_of(philip,edith).
child_of(sylvia,julie).
child_of(sylvia,john).
child_of(max,catherine).

Suppose that to the facts shown above we now wish to add the relation

grandparent(X,Y).

which states that **X** is a grandparent of **Y**. This can be done in two ways: by creating a new set of facts or by defining a rule. It is possible to create new facts yourself from the **child_of** facts given above by working out the grandparent → parent → child relation, or conversely, the child → parent → grandparent relation. We can thus create the following new set of facts to add to the preceding ones:

grandparent(edith,julie).
grandparent(edith,john).
grandparent(philip,sylvia).

and so on.

However, this method of proceeding is very inefficient in terms of memory space because of the redundancy it introduces. Furthermore, the updating of the relation **child_of** will require the updating of all the sets of facts built from this relation. Such extensive updating is likely to be quite complex to handle fully.

2. Constructing a Rule

Another way of proceeding is to introduce a law that says that if there exist variables **X**, **Y**, and **Z** such that there is a fact

child_of(Z,Y).

and such that there is also a fact

child_of(Y,X).

then one may deduce that **X** is the grandparent of **Z**. We thus have two facts to verify at the same time, with a common variable **Y**:

child_of(Z,Y) AND child_of(Y,X).

In logical terms, we say that, if there exist **X**, **Y**, and **Z** such that the condition above is true, then this implies that **X** is the grandparent of **Z**.

This kind of statement is called a *rule*. A rule in Prolog has two parts: the conditions (or constraints) that must be satisfied and the conclusion (or result) that one wishes to deduce. In Prolog the conclusion is shown before the conditions. These two parts are separated by the symbol **:- .** The rule **grandparent(X,Z)** is written

grandparent(X,Z) :- child_of(Z,Y),
                    child_of(Y,X).

In a Prolog rule, the result, shown to the left of the symbol **:-**, is composed of a single predicate. The conditions, given to the right of the symbol **:-**, have the form of a Prolog question. Each part of the condition may be placed on a new line, for the sake of readability. Prolog allows a programmer considerable freedom with regard to the placement of spaces. Only names (of constants, predicates, variables, etc.) may not contain spaces.

The general form of a rule is the following:

a(...) :- b(...), c(...), ... , z(...).

This rule can be paraphrased as **a(...)** is true if and only if **b(...)**, **c(...)**, ..., **z(...)**. is true. Here we represent arguments by **(...)** to indicate that they may be of any nature and number. **a(...)** is called the *head* of the rule and **b(...)**, **c(...)**, ..., **z(...)**. constitutes the *body* of the rule. At a syntactic level, a rule is called a *clause*. The body is also called the *constraints* or the *conditions*. The conditions either make reference to facts or call new rules. If certain variables are bound to constants as a result of a call to a rule, then all occurrences of these variables in the head as well as in the condition part of the rule are bound to the constants for the duration of this particular call to the rule.

Using rules is a general and efficient way of describing information. A rule

. is general because it contains variables,
. is efficient in terms of memory space,
. plays the role of a "super fact".

A Prolog rule expresses a general law, whether or not there are, at a given instant, any solutions to the rule.

Returning to the above example, we shall illustrate several stages of the execution of a rule. Suppose we were to pose the question:

?- grandparent(X,max).

We wish to know which grandparents of Max are known to the fact base. The question cannot be resolved by directly consulting the facts; we must use the rule grandparent, since the fact grandparent does not exist.

The system proceeds as follows:

(1) It immediately tries to unify the question with the head of

the rule **grandparent(,)**. Unification is possible, and **Z** is bound to **max**. This implies that every occurrence of **Z** in the rule is also bound to **max**. The rule then becomes

> **grandparent(X,max) :- child_of(max,Y),**
> **child_of(Y,X).**

(2) The system now tries to prove the condition part of the rule, step by step, by considering the subproblems in the order in which hey appear. It first tries to find a fact (or another rule) that matches **child_of(max,Y)**, and finds **Y = catherine**. All occurrences of **Y** are then rewritten as **catherine**.

(3) The Prolog system attempts to prove the last part of the condition **child_of(catherine,X)**. It finds **X = marcel**.

(4) The value of **X** is propagated automatically to the head of the rule, where **X** has so far remained free. The value of **X** can now be printed.

After unbinding **X**, the system searches for other solutions. This proceeds in exactly the same manner, with the system continuing its traversal of the fact base from the point at which it last stopped.

Using the same procedure as outlined above, we may pose the "inverse" question:

> **?- grandparent(marcel,X).**

which will search for the names of Marcel's grandchildren. The only difference between this new question and the first one is in the call to **grandparent**, where the second argument is a variable, instead of the first.

An interesting feature of Prolog rules is that in posing a question, it is very often possible to instantiate or leave free any of the arguments of the head. This allows the resolution of different kinds of questions with the same rule. We shall return to this point in a subsequent chapter.

To express the relation

> **parent_of(X,Y)**

where **X** is a parent of **Y**, it is possible once again to use the relation **child_of**

> **parent_of(X,Y) :- child_of(Y,X).**

If, furthermore, we know the sex (**masc** or **fem**) of the individuals in the database:

    masc(john).
    masc(jack).
    masc(marcel).
    masc(phillip).
    masc(max).
    fem(catherine).
    fem(edith).
    fem(sylvia).
    fem(martine).
    fem(julie).

then we may also define the relations:

    father_of(X,Y) :- child_of(Y,X),
                    masc(X).

    mother_of(X,Y) :- child_of(Y,X),
                    fem(X).

    grandfather_of(X,Y) :- child_of(Y,Z),
                    child_of(Z,X),
                    masc(X).

    grandmother_of(X,Y) :- child_of(Y,Z),
                    child_of(Z,X),
                    fem(X).

The rule **father_of** may be paraphrased by:

    For all **X** and **Y**, **X** is the father of **Y** if
    (1) **Y** is the child of **X** and
    (2) **X** is of the masculine sex.

The same can be done for the rule **grandfather_of**:

    For all **X** and **Y**, **X** is the grandfather of **Y** if
    (1) there exists a **Z** such that **Y** is the child of **Z** and
    (2) **Z** is the child of **X** and
    (3) **X** is of the masculine sex.

We conclude with some additional examples of rules. To state that John is a friend of all people, we say that for every **X** such that **X** is a person, John is a friend of **X**. This is stated in Prolog as

friend(john,X) :- person(X).

A zoological database might state (superficially) that a bird is an animal that has feathers. This can be expressed as the following rule:

bird(X) :- animal(X), has_feathers(X).

We assume, of course, that the facts **animal(X)** and **has_feathers(X)** are either directly known to the database or deducible from other rules in the system.

3. Rules without Conditions

There is a kind of Prolog rule that does not have a conditional component. These rules can be considered to be facts that have some variable arguments.

Let us assume that we have a fact base that describes individuals. If it contains the relation **know(X,Y)**, which states that **X** knows **Y**, we may then have the following rule:

know(X,X).

which does not contain conditions and which expresses the reflexive character of the relation. It can be paraphrased as "for all **X**, **X** knows himself." Such a rule must be used cautiously, however. If the above database describes not only humans but also objects, it would be useful to add a constraint:

know(X,X) :- person(X).

Other rules without conditions are, for example,

equal(X,X) : **X** is equal to itself.
know(john,X) : John knows every item in the fact base.
possess(john,X) : John possesses every item of the fact base.

4. Rules and Logic

A rule, like a fact, is also a logical axiom. The rule

grandparent(X,Z) :- child_of(Z,Y),
child_of(Y,X).

may be considered to be an implication: if **Z** is a child of **Y** and **Y** is a child of **X**, then **X** is a grandparent of **Z**. Note that the variables in the head of a rule are universally quantified: the preceding rule is true for all values of **X**, **Y**, and **Z** that satisfy the given conditions.

The preceding rule is written in logical notation as follows:

$\forall$ **X, Z,** $\exists$ **Y, child_of(Z,Y)   AND child_of(Y,X)**

$\Rightarrow$ **grandparent(X,Z).**

We describe the logical aspects of Prolog more fully in Chapter 12.

5. Facts and Rules with Complex Arguments

Until now we have been using facts with a simple structure. It is possible to refine the structure of the arguments of a fact by giving them the form of a tree, and not simply of a single constant, as we have been doing.

Two trees are unified in the same way as previously described: by finding equalities between all corresponding elements of the trees. Variables may appear in a tree. A variable may be unified with a subtree.

The use of more highly structured arguments allows information to be grouped and manipulated as a structure, without having to be broken down. This procedure is often used outside of Prolog, for example, for structuring files. We now present a brief example, which does not depend on the Prolog mechanism or on the method of programming.

Here is a "personnel" file whose data are organized in a linear form, without "in-depth" structuring:

personnel(Last_name,
First_name,
Age,
Number_of_children,

```
                        Rank,
                        Seniority).
```

Here is the same file with structured data:

```
personnel(identification(Last_name,
                        First_name,Age),
                        Number_of_children,
                        status(Rank,Seniority)).
```

The choice of how to structure data depends on the problem that is being solved.

Using such a data structure, we can profitably make use of the technique of *data abstraction*, which consists of structuring the data and defining simple and general means of accessing them.

For example, we may define the following rule from the structured fact shown above:

```
situation(Last_name,Rank)  :-
                        personnel(identification
                        (Last_name,_,_),_,
                        status(Rank,_)).
```

The symbol _ means that this argument is not relevant to the problem at hand and will not be the object of a unification.

It is also possible to associate several types of facts to create a new data type. Thus, to obtain a list of the male personnel, we could write

```
male_personnel(Last_name,First_name)  :-
                        personnel(identification(Last_name,
                        First_name,_),_,_),
                        masc(First_name).
```

Data abstraction is not peculiar to Prolog; it is, however, particularly easy to express in this language.

6. Summary

The first three chapters have presented the syntax and the principal basic concepts of Prolog. Remember that:

. The objects that are manipulated are facts, rules, and questions.

. Facts contain information that is unconditionally true.

. Rules allow the definition of new concepts from facts or other rules. The use of rules is particularly efficient in terms of memory space and provides a means of expression more powerful than classical data types.

. The user can interrogate a knowledge base by asking questions.

Exercises

Ex. 3.1

From the data given in Section 3.1, define the following rules:

(a) **daughter_of(X,Y).**
(b) **great_grandfather(X,Y).**
(c) **great_grandmother(X,Y).**

Ex. 3.2

Write the Prolog rules corresponding to

(1) John knows every person who knows him,
(2) John knows all the friends of Pierre,
(3) the friends of my friends are my friends.

by using the relations given in this chapter and the relation **friend(X,Y)**, which says that **X** has **Y** for a friend.

Ex. 3.3

From the following types of facts:

course(Prof_name,Course_number).
student(Student_name,Number_of_course_taken).

define:

student_of(Student_name,Prof_name).

Also write the rule which states that each student knows the professor who teaches a course that he is taking.

Chapter 4

Syntax of Prolog.
The Unification Mechanism

In this chapter we describe the syntax of the basic concepts of Prolog presented so far. This chapter is not essential to understanding Prolog; it simply permits us to establish certain definitions. We first propose some intuitive definitions, which we then complete with formal definitions for those readers familiar with formal grammars.

Prolog manipulates elementary objects (*atoms, numbers,* and *variables*) and structured objects (*terms*). Facts and rules are called *clauses. Facts* are clauses with an empty body.

1. Numbers and Atoms

Numbers in Prolog include positive and negative integers and real numbers:

12   -17   0.143   -13.456

Certain versions of Prolog are limited to positive integers. This is due to the fact that real numbers are not frequently used in Prolog, which is a language designed primarily for symbolic deduction. However, they prove very useful for database applications. Real numbers can lead to complex unification problems because they must be rounded off to fit in the computer's finite memory.

An atom is an *identifier*: the name of a constant, a predicate, or an operator. Atoms can take a very large number of forms, including upper- and lowercase letters (except at the beginning of a word), numbers (but always accompanied by other characters), and special characters such as +, -, <, =, etc. Here are some examples of atoms:

> **john   a22   j_817A   the_magic_flute**
> **<:>**
> **:: =**

The use of single quotation marks allows the use of constants beginning with a capital letter, such as

> **'Max'.**

2. Variables

A variable is represented by a symbol composed of a sequence of characters, numbers, and underline characters (low dashes). A variable symbol always begins with a capital letter or an underline character:

> **Begin**
> **String2**
> **X Y Z**
> **Result_C**
> **_521**

When variables in a rule play no role (i.e., they appear only once), they may be replaced by an underline character which prevents Prolog from making useless unifications. The underline indicates that the argument exists but is of no present interest. Thus when we define

> **parent(Y) :- child_of(X,Y).**

X is of no particular interest in this rule (we are interested only in its existence, not in its value). Thus, we write

> **parent(Y) :- child_of(_,Y).**

3. Terms

Numbers, constants, and variables in a program are called terms. A tree is a term; it is a structure composed of numbers, constants, and variables:

> **father_of(X,Y)**
> **known(X,father(alan,mark),Z1)**
> **_1544**
> **spot**

The root of the tree is called the *head* or *main functor* of the term. In the term

> **a(b(c,d1),Z,Y)**

a is the main functor because it is the root of the tree below it. In turn, this term is composed of three arguments which may each be a term (**b(c,d1)**) or an atom (**Z** and **Y**). Finally, we say that the arity of the term whose head is **a** is 3 because it contains three arguments. The arity of the subterm **b(c,d1)** is 2.

A term is said to be completely instantiated (or ground) if it does not contain any variables. For example,

> **g(1,a1(U,_12))**

is not completely instantiated because it contains two variables, **U** and **_12**, whereas

> **g(1,a1(34,op))**

is a completely instantiated term.

Note also that in most versions of Prolog, functors in a term must not be variables. The term **X(a,b)** is not accepted by Prolog, and neither, for example, is the term **f(X(a,b),c)**.

To overcome this problem, we can create a supplementary functor with a new name and include **X** among its arguments. In the following example **f1** is such a functor:

> **f(f1(X,a,b),c)**

4. Clauses

A rule is called a clause at the syntactic level. The general form of a clause is

    a(...) :- b(...), ..., z(...).

where **a(...)** is called the *head literal* of the clause (or, simply, the head of the clause) and **b(...), ..., z(...).** constitutes the *body* of the clause (the constraints); they are also literals.

a(...), **b(...)** and **z(...)** are terms. Their arguments are also terms and may be simple or complex. **b(...), ..., z(...).** are calls to facts or other rules. When the clause **a** is called, the following actions take place:

(1) unification of the question **a(...)** with the head of the clause,
(2) attempts to prove first **b**, then all the following conditions in the order in which they are written, all the way to **z**.

Variables contained in a clause are local to this clause, just like the variables in Pascal procedures. By way of illustration, consider the following two clauses,

    a(X) :- b(X).
    c(X) :- f(X),g(X,_).

in which variable **X** in the first clause is independent of **X** in the second clause. During the course of the interpretation of a program by Prolog, new variables are created to avoid any conflict between variables with the same name. This renaming is accomplished by variables of the form _**123**, _**124**, and so on. Thus, the two preceding clauses become

    a(_1) :- b(_1).
    c(_2) :- f(_2),g(_2,_).

5. Formal Definitions of Terms and Clauses

For the reader experienced in the formal expression of grammars, here is the grammar that describes the syntax of a term and a clause:

<canonical term> ::= <variable> /
    <canonical functional term>
<canonical functional term> := <functional symbol> /
    <functional symbol> (<list of canonical terms>)
<variable> ::= <non reserved unit>
<functional symbol> ::= <non reserved unit>
<list of canonical terms> ::= <canonical term> /
    <canonical term>, <list of canonical terms>

<clause> ::= <head literal> :- <sequence of calls> /
    <head literal>
<head literal ::= <predicate name> (<list of terms>)
<list of terms> ::= <canonical term>, <list of terms> /
    <canonical term>
<sequence of calls> ::= <called literal>, <sequence of calls> /
    <called literal>
<called literal> ::= <predicate name> (<list of terms>)

6. Substitutions

Substitution is the basic operation of the unification mechanism. To substitute a variable by a term is to replace all the occurrences of the variable by the term. Note carefully that it is a variable that is replaced by a term, and not the opposite. To avoid infinite loops, it is necessary that the term that replaces a variable does not contain any occurrences of this variable. That is, there must be no substitutions of the type

$$X \; \text{->} \; f(...,X,...).$$

If this case arises, it is necessary to rename the X in f. If this is not done, we can substitute X an infinite number of times with $f(...X...)$, which gives

$$f(...f(...f(...f(...f(...)))))).$$

Consider the substitution $S(X,T)$, which replaces all the occurrences of variable X with the term T in another term. For example,

$$S(X,a(b,Z)) \text{ applied to the term } V = b(X,g(Y,X))$$

results in

$$S(V) = b(a(b,Z),\ g(Y,a(b,Z))).$$

This can be seen clearly if the terms are written as trees.

S replaces **X** with

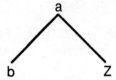

The term **V** is written

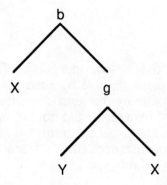

Once the substitution is made, **V** becomes

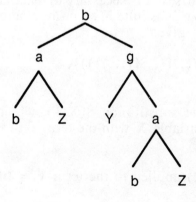

Note that the substitution $S(X,a(b,Z))$ applied to **T1** = **f(Y,Z)** leaves **T1** unchanged because **T1** does not contain any occurrence of the variable **X**.

7. Unification of Terms

Two terms **T** and **U** are unifiable if and only if there exist one or several substitutions that, applied simultaneously to **T** and **U**, make these two terms identical. If such a set of substitutions does not exist, the two terms are not unifiable. For example, consider the terms **T** and **U**:

T = **p(X, f(a,b), g(Z,F))**
U = **p(t(e), W, g(3,C))**

If we apply the following group **S** of substitutions to **T** and **U**,

S = **{S1(X,t(e)), S2(W,f(a,b)), S3(Z,3),**
S4(F,C)}

both **T** and **U** become the following term:

p(t(e), f(a,b), g(3,C))

which consequently means that **T** and **U** are unifiable. Note that the substitution **S4** is simply a renaming of variable **F**. **F** and **C** are called *alphabetic variants*.

Unification is the fundamental operation of Prolog. It permits the manipulation and transfer of data, as well as the expression of constraints on data, through the use of several occurrences of the same variable in a clause. Unification also allows us to determine, with the aid of substitutions, wether two trees (i.e., terms) or subtrees are identical.

Unification enables us to access different subconstituents of a term through the use of variables that can be unified with a part of a term. For example, to extract **a(b,c)** from the term **t(c,a(b,c), Y)**, we can simply unify this term with the term **t(_,X,_)** and **X** is bound to **a(b,c)**. **X** can then be used in the remainder of the clause to carry along the term that it is bound to.

A term **T** is an instance of a term **U** if there exists a substitution (or a group of substitutions) **S** such that

T = S(U)

T is the result of the application of **S** to **U**. We also say that **T** is less general than **U**.

The algorithm that determines wether two terms are unifiable is fairly complex because each argument of a term may itself be a term. It is not necessary to know this algorithm to program in Prolog. The reader can refer to works cited in the Bibliography for more information. The exercises given at the end of the chapter provide the opportunity to gain familiarity with the unification mechanism.

Exercises

Ex. 4.1

Apply the substitution **S(X,a(b,c(e,Y)))** to the terms

(a) **T1 = f(X,X)**,
(b) **T2 = g(f(X),h(X,3))**,
(c) **T3 = u(X,f(Y,X))**.

Represent **T1**, **T2**, and **T3** as trees before and after applying the substitution.

Ex. 4.2

State whether the following terms are unifiable. If so, give the substitutions that must be applied:

(a) **T = f(a,f(b,c))** and **U = f(X,Y)**,
(b) **T = f(a,f(a,b))** and **U = g(X,Z)**,
(c) **T = plus(f(a,b),c)** and **U = plus(X,X)**,
(d) **T = f(X,h(T,Y))** and **U = f(Z,h(a,n(W)))**.

Hint: for each pair of terms, proceed step by step from the leftmost to the rightmost arguments.

Chapter 5

Arithmetic Operations

The first part of this chapter introduces arithmetic and logical operators. The second part develops a concrete example of querying databases where these operators are used.

1. Arithmetic Operators

Because Prolog is essentially a language dedicated to symbolic deduction, its facilities for numerical calculations are at present rather modest. In certain versions these facilities are insufficient and make the system unsuitable for real use.

The usual arithmetic operators are the following:

+	addition
-	subtraction
*	multiplication
/	division
mod	remainder after division by an integer

To bind a variable to a value of an arithmetic expression, it is necessary to use the operator **is**. To the question

?- X is 3-2.

Prolog responds:

X = 1

Parentheses can be used in the usual way:

?- X is (3*2) - 1.
X = 5
?- X is 14 - (10/2).

X = 9

It is possible to use variables on the right-hand side of the operator **is**, but they must be instantiated before the execution of the operation. Otherwise, an error results. For example, we can define the rule **incr(X,Y)**, which increments **X** by **1** and puts the result in **Y**, as shown below:

incr(X,Y) :- Y is X + 1.

In this case, the variable **X** must be instantiated for any call of **incr(X,Y)**, as in the following example:

?- incr(12,Y).
Y = 13

More complex operations can be defined from these basic operators. Examples are presented in the following chapters. We now define the operation that finds the average of four numbers, **X1**, **X2**, **X3**, and **X4**:

average(X1, X2, X3, X4, R) :-
R is (X1 + X2 + X3 + X4) / 4.

Unlike in a classical programming language, it is not possible for Prolog to place the result of the calculation in **X1**, for example, instead of using a new variable. During the execution of the operation **average**, **X1**, **X2**, **X3**, and **X4** must be instantiated; the value of **X1** cannot be modified to hold the result of the calculation. Because of this, Prolog requires the use of a greater number of variables than other languages. However, the role and significance of each variable is simpler and more easily understood.

2. Logical Operators

Logical operators allow different values to be compared. These values may be expressed directly or by means of variables. The usual operators are

X > Y	**X** is greater than **Y**
X < Y	**X** is less than **Y**
X >= Y	**X** is greater than or equal to **Y**
X =< Y	**X** is less than or equal to **Y**
X =\= Y	**X** is different from **Y**

To the question

?- 120 >= 12.

Prolog responds:

yes

When variables are used in a logical expression, they must be instantiated before the application of the logical operator. If not, the comparison is not valid; comparing two unbound variables or a free variable with a value is meaningless.

In addition to the logical operators that work on numbers, there are three logical operators that work on terms:

X = **Y** is true if **X** unifies with **Y**.
X == **Y** is true if **X** and **Y** have exactly the same structure, argument for argument.
X \== **Y** is true if **X** and **Y** do not have exactly the same structure.

By "exactly the same structure," we mean that the tree represented by **X** covers exactly the tree represented by **Y**, and vice versa.

For simple equality (=), it is sufficient that **X** and **Y** be unifiable, that is, that a variable in **X** can be unified with a subtree in **Y** and equality preserved.

In the case of "strong" equality (==), wherever there is a constant in **X**, the same constant must exist in **Y**, and wherever there is a variable in **X**, there must be a variable in **Y**, modulo the renaming of the variables.

Finally, the operator **is**, which binds a variable to the result of a calculation, must not be confused with **equal**, which is a logical operator that simply makes a comparison.

3. Application to Databases

Our sample database contains very simple information about flight reservations. The general form of a fact is

```
flight(flight_number,
       departing_from,
       destination,
       departure_time,
       arrival_time,
       number_of_reservations).
```

Examples:

```
flight(1,toronto,montreal,1200,1300,42).
flight(2,saskatoon,toronto,1400,1525,245).
flight(3,toronto,ottawa,1345,1500,234).
flight(4,vancouver,calgary,0920,1100,51).
flight(5,montreal,halifax,1030,1250,58).
```

The last example means that there is a flight (number 5) from Montreal to Halifax, departing at 10:30 (hours and minutes have been concatenated, so only whole numbers are used), arriving at 12:50, and carrying 58 passengers with reservations.

We now demonstrate how to write questions in Prolog that

    (a) give the list of flights (the number of the flight is sufficient) departing from Saskatoon,
    (b) give the list of flights that arrive in Toronto,
    (c) give the list of flights departing from Montreal that leave before 12:00,
    (d) give the list of flights leaving from any city that arrive after 2:00 p.m. (14:00 on the 24-hour clock),
    (e) give the list of flights with more than 100 passengers that arrive at Montreal up to 5:00 p.m. (17:00),
    (f) give the list of flights that leave at the same time from any two cities and also, the names of these cities in the order in which they appear,
    (g) give the list of flights that last longer than 2 hours and depart from any city.

These questions are formulated as follows:

    (a) ?- flight(X,saskatoon,_,_,_,_).

To indicate that the flight departs from Saskatoon, the constant **saskatoon** is given in the question. We could also write

    ?- flight(X,X2,_,_,_,_), X2 = saskatoon.

but this is more cumbersome. The question is only unified with facts that have saskatoon as the value of the second argument.

(b) **?- flight(X,_,toronto,_,_,_).**

(c) **?- flight(X,montreal,_,Y,_,_), Y<1200.**

In this case it is not possible to write the constraint **Y<1200** in the argument corresponding to the departure time. We therefore add a constraint to the question.

(d) **?- flight(X,_,_,_,Z,_), Z >= 1400.**

(e) **?- flight(X,_,montreal,_,Z,P), Z=<1700, P>100.**

Note the use of two selection constraints in question (e). The two possible orders in which these constraints may be given are logically equivalent. In terms of the time the query takes to execute, the order of the constraints may lead to slight differences in efficiency. In order to concentrate as soon as possible on likely solutions, it is better to place the most restrictive constraint first. This enables us to reduce the amount of backtracking Prolog does while finding the solutions.

(f) **?- flight(X,V1,_,Y,_,_), flight(A,V2,_,Y,_,_).**

Note here that **Y** has been used in two places to force equality of the arguments. To obtain good-looking output, the command **write(X)** should be followed by the command **write(' ')**, to leave several spaces. Note that the same response to this query is obtained several times. This is because Prolog tries all possible proofs of the two calls to flight without remembering which it has already done. Of course, it never does exactly the same proof twice. There are techniques for making Prolog remember the actions it has already done, in particular, by using lists. This is explained in Chapter 14. For similar reasons, we also obtain answers consisting of two flights leaving from the same city at the same time (in other words, two identical flights!). To avoid this, the predicate **diff** (whose implementation we shall soon see) may be used with the call **diff(Y1,Y2)**, to ensure that the two cities are different:

?- flight(X,Y1,_,Y,_,_), flight(A,Y2,_,Y,_,_), diff(Y1,Y2).

(g) ?- flight(X,_,_,D,A,_), A - D >200.

More complex examples are given in the chapter devoted to deductive databases. The concepts of lists and recursion, however, need to be introduced first.

Chapter 6

Procedures

We now introduce a very interesting peculiarity of Prolog: the ability to define several rules (or clauses) with the same head. This technique allows us to state independently different possible ways of proving a goal, when several ways exist.

1. The Problem

We hope to define the rule

max(X,Y,R)

which binds **R** to the larger of two numbers **X** and **Y**. If **X** is equal to **Y**, then **X** is chosen. We may then say that

R = X if X ≥ Y,
R = Y if Y > X.

This rule cannot be expressed with a single clause because we cannot express disjunctions of cases. We are thus led to propose two definitions for **max** with mutually exclusive conditions:

```
max(X,Y,X) :- X >= Y.
max(X,Y,Y) :- Y > X.
```

We require two clauses to define **max**. Several clauses with the same head predicate form a *procedure*. Note that the order of the two clauses in procedure **max** can be changed without affecting the value of the result. The condition parts of the two clauses that define **max** are composed of calls to predefined Prolog predicates (>= or >). The condition part of a clause can contain calls to facts, rules, and predefined predicates.

Note the way in which the result is expressed: the third

argument of **max** directly contains either **X** or **Y**, depending on the case. Another possibility might be

    max(X,Y,R) :- X >= Y, R is X.
    max(X,Y,R) :- Y > X, R is Y.

This is needlessly cumbersome, however, because **R** does not play any role other than holding the result. It is thus preferable to write the result directly, using **X** or **Y**. An example of a call to **max** is

    ?- max(12,4,X).

The response is

    X = 12

Note that the variables remain local to each clause; there are no global variables.

2. Procedures

A procedure groups together a set of clauses that have the same term (same name, same number of arguments) as the head of the clause:

    a(X) :- b(X,_).
    a(X) :- c(X),e(X).
    a(X) :- f(X,_).

This procedure contains three clauses with head **a(X)**. Each clause of a procedure expresses one way of solving **a(X)**. The example above may be paraphrased as **a(X)** is true if **b(X,_)** is true OR if **c(X)** AND **e(X)** are true OR if **f(X,_)** is true. In a procedure there is an implicit OR between each clause. This is an innovation in comparison with classical programming languages, where two procedures may not have the same name. Note also the contrast with the conditions in a clause, which are bound by an implicit AND, represented by a comma.

In the example given in the preceding paragraph, the two clauses in the procedure **max** are mutually exclusive. This is not an inherent property of clauses in a procedure. Each clause is merely one way of defining a property, a relation, a situation, and so on, and there is therefore no reason for the different clauses to exclude each other. Thus a bird, for example, may be defined as

```
bird(X) :- fly(X).
bird(X) :- has_feathers(X).
bird(X) :- has_a_beak(X).
```

It is also possible to group two clauses of the same procedure into a single clause to condense the writing. For example, the two clauses

```
a(X) :- b(X,Y), c(X), d(Y,Z).
a(X) :- b(X,Y), g(X,Z), d(Y,Z).
```

may be condensed by using a semicolon, which represents an implicit OR:

```
a(X) :- b(X,Y), (c(X); g(X,Z)), d(Y,Z).
```

This notation is useful particularly when two clauses have very similar conditional parts.

3. Execution Order of Clauses in a Procedure

Theoretically, the order of clauses in a procedure is unimportant. This is, however, no longer true when, for reasons of efficiency, we wish to influence Prolog's internal control. In this case we must pay careful attention to the order of the clauses. This idea is developed further when we deal with suppressing the remaining choices.

From an operational point of view, when a procedure is called, Prolog executes the clauses one after another, starting with the first (a completely arbitrary choice, but a necessary one when using sequential machines). If Prolog fails to prove a clause, it passes on to the following clause and continues in this manner until it reaches the last clause. If all of the attempted proofs of all the clauses in the procedure fail, the result is false; no clause is provable for the given call. For the result to be true, at least one of the clauses of the procedure must be true.

As soon as a clause is proved, the system continues its work. However, in the event of backtracking or attempts at finding another solution, the system may execute other clauses of the procedure. The system remembers which clauses of a particular procedure it has not yet examined at each point of the proof. This is realized by means of a list, associated with each node of the proof tree that contains remaining choices that can be used to build the current proof. If there are several ways of solving a problem, Prolog will try them all.

At the level of a procedure, when Prolog analyzes a program, it creates a pointer (or entry point) for each procedure. It then numbers each clause of every procedure according to its order of appearance. This numbering is used during the execution of a program: clauses are executed in the order in which they are numbered within each procedure. If we have the program

    c :- a,b.
    c :- d.
    c :- e,a.

Prolog will produce the following enumeration for the procedure **c**:

    (1) c :- a,b.
    (2) c :- d.
    (3) c :- e,a.

The entry point in the procedure is clause (1). During the execution of a program, a call to **c** starts the execution of the procedure **c** in the order determined above.

Suppose that **a**, **b**, **d**, and **e** are procedures defined in the program:

(1) The call to **c** initiates an attempt to prove the first clause, which leads to an attempt to prove first **a** and then **b**, taking into account any substitutions made during the unification of the call to **c** with this clause (when there are arguments).

(2) In case of failure during (1) or a request to find another possible solution to the problem, Prolog attempts a proof of the second clause, which requires a proof of **d**, under the same conditions as above. This process continues.

(3) After examining the last clause of procedure **c**, there is a failure if none of the clauses of the procedure can be proved.

In Chapter 8 we examine in more depth the interactions between different procedures. Associated control mechanisms employed in Prolog are also introduced.

4. Procedures and Classical Programming

The contribution of a procedure to a Prolog program is comparable to that of a procedure or subroutine in a program written in a classical programming language. Like a classical procedure, a Prolog procedure gives a complete way of finding a solution to a problem. It can also be viewed more declaratively as providing the complete definition of a property or relation. Consequently, two Prolog procedures may not have the same head predicate.

A procedure may be seen as a classical *if...then...else...* structure, or more generally, as a case structure. This Prolog case structure is weaker than the classical one in the sense that cases are not necessarily mutually exclusive. The program for **max** may be written as follows in pseudo-Pascal:

max(X,Y,R);

case:
$X \geq Y \rightarrow R := X,$
$X < Y \rightarrow R := Y$
endcase;

Similarly, the definition of a bird can be given as

case:
fly(X) $\rightarrow$ **bird(X),**
has_feathers(X) $\rightarrow$ **bird(X),**
has_a_beak(X) $\rightarrow$ **bird(X)**
endcase;

The examples presented in this section and the questions that they raise are more relevant to the general modeling of knowledge than to programming in Prolog. However, the use of Prolog has consequences with regard to the way definitions and relations are expressed. We return to this point in the second part of this book, which is dedicated to applications.

Exercises

Ex. 6.1

Write the procedure **larger(X,N)**, which writes the value of **X** if **X** is larger than **N**, and the value of **N** if not.

Ex. 6.2

Write the procedure **sum_diff(X,Y,Z)**, which places in **Z** the sum of **X** and **Y** if **X** is greater than **Y**, and the difference between **X** and **Y** if not.

Ex. 6.3

Extend the above procedure by adding the following restriction: if **X** is strictly negative, then place the value of **Y** in **Z**.

Chapter 7

Recursion

Recursion is a method of programming frequently used in Prolog. It is not unique to Prolog; it may also be used in classical programming languages such as Pascal. However, since it is used much more frequently in Prolog (instead of loops), and in a characteristic way, it is useful to dedicate a chapter to it.

1. Recursion and Recurrence

Recursion is directly inspired by the *recurrence* relations that one encounters in mathematics, with the difference that a recursive process is always a finite process. A recurrent schema is composed of three parts:

. an initial condition, to start the process,
. a development scheme that expresses the recurrence,
. a stop condition, optional in mathematics because infinite processes can be handled.

An elementary use of recurrence is the definition of sequences of elements. For example, the sequence of the first 10 whole even numbers is

0 2 4 6 8 10 12 14 16 18.

The recurrent schema that constructs this sequence is as follows:

The initial condition is the element at the beginning of the sequence, here **0**. Let us call it the current element. The development plan used to construct the sequence consists of defining, from the current element, the succeeding element:

next element = current element + 2

The next element then becomes the current element, and the process continues. The process stops when 10 elements have been defined.

The concept of level is associated with the development plan. At the initial stage, which is called, for example, stage **0**, the current element is **0** and **next element = current element + 2 = 0 + 2 = 2.** The next element of level **0** becomes the current element of level **1: current element = 2.** At level **2**, the current element is then **4**, etc. We can use the level number as an index. We then no longer need to refer to the current element and to the next element at each level since:

next element (i)   = current element (i) + 2
= current element (i + 1).

We now have the relation

current element (i + 1) = current element (i) + 2.

This relation is called the recurrence relation. The end of the calculation will be just before the calculation of current element **(10)**, since the levels are numbered from **0** to **9**.

Recursion is expressed in a similar fashion to recurrence. It also comprises three elements:

. an initial condition, given in Prolog by the call to a recursive procedure,
. a development plan, which in Prolog contains the recursive call,
. a stop condition, often expressed by another procedure.

A clause containing a recursive call is a clause that contains in its body at least one call to itself:

a(X) :- b(X,Y), a(Y).

Since the clause **a** calls itself, it executes indefinitely, and we have an infinite loop. A simple solution to this problem is to add a stop condition, expressed by another clause with head **a**. This clause, called the stop condition, must be examined before each new recursive call, a requirement that implies that it must be the first call of the procedure. Other stopping techniques are examined in Chapter 9, which is dedicated to lists.

To illustrate recursion in Prolog, we return to the writing of the first 10 whole even numbers. We assume the predicate

number(X,E), where **X** designates an element of the sequence being constructed, and **E** the level number. The recursive schema is the following:

> **number(X,E) :- write(X),**
> **E 1 is E + 1,**
> **X 1 is X + 2,**
> **number(X1,E1).**

The stop condition is given using the level number **E**:

> **number(X,10).**

The procedure is invoked with the call

> **?- number(0,0).**

We thus have a recursive procedure composed of two clauses. However, so that the stop condition will be considered during each new call to number, it must be the first clause of the procedure. Otherwise, it will never be called, and the program will loop indefinitely. The number procedure becomes

> **number(X,10).**
> **number(X,E) :- write(X),**
> **E 1 is E + 1,**
> **X 1 is X + 2,**
> **number(X1,E1).**

Recursion may be expressed in a less direct fashion than the example above. It may occur through an intermediary of two or more different procedures:

> **a(1).**
> **a(X) :- b(X).**
> **b(X) :- X1 is X - 2, a(X1).**

Procedure **a** calls **b**, which again calls **a**. This is also a recursive system.

Recursion in a clause may take two forms:

(1) *right recursion*, as in the example

> **a(X) :- b(X,Y), a(X).**

where the call to **a(X)** is the end of the clause. This is the most popular form, and it is also the simplest to control.

(2) *left recursion*, as in

a(X) :- a(X), b(Y,2).

where the call to **a(X)** is at the beginning of the clause. This form must be used with caution to avoid infinite loops. We shall see more examples of this in Chapter 9.

2. Paths in a Graph

We now develop a more complex example: determining the existence of one (or several) paths between two nodes of a graph. Consider, for example, the following graph:

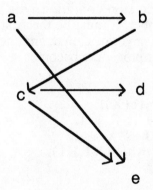

An *arc* expresses a relation between two nodes. It is therefore natural to represent a graph in Prolog by facts in the form **arc(X,Y)** to state the existence of an arc from **X** to **Y**, where **X** and **Y** are nodes of the graph. The above graph is expressed as follows:

```
arc(a,b).
arc(b,c).
arc(c,e).
arc(c,d).
arc(a,e).
```

We now wish to know wether there exists at least one path from node **a** to node **d**. We use the call

?- path(a,d).

We define the predicate **path(X,Y)** to be evaluated as true if a path exists between **X** and **Y**. The problem breaks down into two cases, expressed by two clauses for the procedure **path**. The first clause treats the case in which the path is elementary: there is a path between two points if there is an arc that joins them. The second clause treats the case in which the path is not elementary: there is a path from **X** to **Y** if there exists a **Z** such that there is an arc from **X** to **Z** and a path from **Z** to **Y**.

We thus define a recursive schema. The elementary case is characterized by the existence of an arc joining **X** to **Y**. In the general case we assume that the problem at the lower levels has been solved (here, there is a path from **Z** to **Y**), and the rule treats the problem at the immediately higher level (here, by adding an arc to the path already supposedly known). The program is written

> **path(X,Y)** :- **arc(X,Y)**.
> **path(X,Y)** :- **arc(X,Z)**, **path(Z,Y)**.

Let us examine the execution of the question

> **?- path(a,d)**.

Prolog numbers the clauses of the procedure **path** according to the order in which they are written. This order will also correspond to the order of execution:

> (1) **path(X,Y)** :- **arc(X,Y)**.
> (2) **path(X,Z)** :- **arc(X,Y)**, **path(Y,Z)**.

The execution process is shown below:

> Level 1:
>
> clause number 1: **path(X,Y)** :- **arc(X,Y)**.
> unification with the call
>
> **path(a,d)** :- **arc(a,d)**. → FAILURE
>
> clause number 2: **path(X,Z)** :- **arc(X,Y)**, **path(Y,Z)**.
> unification with the call
>
> **path(a,d)** :- **arc(a,Y)**, **path(Y,d)**.

The fact **arc(a,b)** permits the unification: **Y = b**. The goal:

path(b,d) must now be proved if **path(a,d)** is to be shown true. The call proceeds in exactly the same way, as shown in Level 2.

Level 2:

clause number 1: **path(X,Y) :- arc(X,Y).**
unification with the call

path(b,d) :- arc(b,d). → FAILURE

clause number 2, after unification with the call

path(b,d) :- arc(b,Y), path(Y,d).

The fact **arc(b,c)** permits the unification of **Y** with **c**. The recursive call is **path(c,d)**. This call is described as Level 3.

Level 3:

clause number 1: **path(X,Y) :- arc(X,Y).**
unification with the call

path(c,d) :- arc(c,d). → SUCCESS

Now that the call at level 3 is proved, it follows that the recursive call at level 2 is also proved since there are no other conditions left to prove. In the same way, and for the same reasons, the recursive call at level 1 is proved by the successful proof of the call

?- path(a,d).

The series of recursive calls is terminated; since there are no literals in the preceding calls awaiting execution after this call, it follows that the entire question has been answered. When there are other solutions, Prolog searches for all of them. This would be the case if, for example, the fact **arc(b,d).** is added. There are now two ways of proving that there is a path from **a** to **d**, depending on which of paths **a → b → c → d** and **a → b → d** is considered. There can, however, also be an infinite loop if there is a cycle in the graph.

Note that the **path** program does not give the path that must be followed to go from **X** to **Y**. It simply indicates wether or not a path exists. This program could be slightly modified to make the path that joins **X** to **Y** more explicit. This would require a list, a structure that we shall see in Chapter 9.

The program given above for finding a path in a graph may appear arbitrary. We could also have written, for example,

path(X,Y) :- arc(X,Y).
path(X,Y) :- path(X,Z), arc(Z,Y).

which is logically equivalent to the preceding program. However, when we consider the execution strategy of clauses in Prolog, it appears that the second clause introduces an infinite loop because **Z** remains free until the execution of **arc(Z,Y)**. This execution will not take place until the calls to **path** terminate.

If Prolog were to use another execution strategy, *breadth-first* search, for example, there would be no loop in this particular case. When writing a recursive clause, two factors must be kept in mind:

(1) the logical formulation of the problem,
(2) the manner in which the program will be executed. This point is developed in the following chapter.

There are other ways to use the **path** program, depending on whether the arguments are free or instantiated. If the first argument is left free, as in the call

?- path(X,d).

Prolog gives the set of nodes **X** of the graph from which there exists a path to **d**, since Prolog gives all the solutions to a problem. If the second argument is freed,

?- path(a,X).

Prolog gives all the nodes **X** that are accessible from **a**. Finally, if both arguments are free, Prolog gives all the paths, of all lengths, that exist in the graph.

3. Calculating the Length of a Path

Suppose that we now wish to know not only the existence of a path, but also its length, expressed as the number of arcs crossed to go from the initial node to the final one. In our example the length of the path from node **a** to node **d** is three arcs. To write the program, we reason in the following way:

(1) If the path from one point to another is elementary, its length is 1. We thus add a third argument to the clause path:

path(X,Y,L).

where **L** designates the length of the path from **X** to **Y**. For an elementary path, we have the clause

path(X,Y,1) :- arc(X,Y).

(2) For a nonelementary path from **X** to **Y**, let **L1** be the length of the path from **Z** to **Y**. If there is an arc from **X** to **Z**, the length of the path from **X** to **Y** is

L = L1 + 1.

The program is written

path(X,Y,1) :- arc(X,Y).
path(X,Y,L) :- arc(X,Z), path(Z,Y,L1), L is L1 + 1.

L is calculated after the recursive call, because **L1** must be instantiated before the addition.

In this program, unlike in the preceding one, there is an operation that must be carried out after the recursive call to **path.** This operation will be carried out in the reverse order to that of the recursive calls because it is executed after **path**. The first path length is known only after the recursive calls have been finished:

path(c,d,1).

Thus, after **path(c,d,1)** is proved, Prolog executes **L is L1 + 1** from level 2. At this level, the value of **L1** is known: **L1 = 1.**

path(b,d,L) :- arc(b,c), path(c,d,1), L is 1 + 1.

At this level, **L = 2**, there are two arcs between **b** and **d.** Finally, and for the same reasons:

path(a,d,L) :- arc(a,b), path(b,d,2), L is 2 + 1.

At this level, **L = 3.** To the question

?- path(a,d,L).

Prolog responds

L = 3.

Prolog manages recursion by a relatively classical stack mechanism. Since every stack has a limited size, the system must watch to ensure that it does not exceed a certain number of calls (generally several hundred) in order to keep the stacks from overflowing. If the number of recursive calls for a complex problem risks becoming too high, it is better to break the problem into several parts. The stack is emptied after the final return from each series of recursive calls.

Exercises

Ex. 7.1

Write a recursive program **table(N)** that, when called, produces a multiplication table for **N**. For example, with **N = 4**,

?- table(4).

It will produce a multiplication table for **4**, starting with **1 * 4** and finishing with **10 * 4**. (The output format is "10 times 4 = 40".)

Ex. 7.2

From the relation **child_of(X,Y)**, define the relation **ancestor_of(X,Y)**, where **X** is an ancestor of **Y**. Modify the program to show the number of generations that separate **X** from **Y**.

Ex. 7.3

Write a program that interactively reads a nonnull set of numbers one after the other, calculating the sum step by step, and then prints the average of these numbers when it reads the end-of-output marker **0**. The call is **average**. A number is read using the predefined predicate **read(X)**, which assumes that each data item is terminated by a period.The drafting of this program generally requires two stages and thus two different procedures.

Chapter 8

Structure and Management of Control

In this chapter we examine with more precision resolution mechanisms in Prolog. We present simplified data structures underlying those mechanisms and show how it is possible to intervene in the proof procedure.

The mechanisms that govern the resolution of a problem are called the *control mechanisms* of the resolution. Some knowledge, even superficial, of these mechanisms is necessary for efficient programming in Prolog.

We next present predefined predicates that allow the programmer to intervene in the control and the problem resolution. Finally, we study negation in Prolog.

1. Control Structure

During the execution of a question, the Prolog system manages calls to clauses, unification, and backtracking. We say that the Prolog system controls the execution of the query or the demonstration of the goal.

If we were to stop the execution at a given instant, the different tasks already performed and those to be performed could be classified in one of three categories:

. the proven goals,
. the goals in the process of being proved.
. the goals that remain to be proved.

Moreover, each goal that is already proved has associated with it, in the proof tree, a list of clauses in the procedure that have not yet been considered by the execution in progress. We call this list *the list of remaining choices*. This list contains the numbers of the clauses not yet used in the attempted demonstration of the procedure being considered. For example, consider the following program, where we have numbered the clauses to facilitate comprehension.

(1) a :- c, d.
(2) a :- a.

(1) c :- d, a.
(2) c :- e.
(3) c :- e, c.

(1) e :- d, f.
(2) e.

(1) d :- f.
(2) d :- d, f.

(1) f :- a.
(2) f :- c.
(3) f :- d, e, f.
(4) f :- a, d.

Consider the call

t :- a, b.

We place ourselves at an arbitrary point in the development of the proof, which we represent by the following tree:

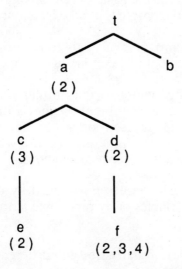

For goal **a**, choice 2 has not yet been considered. For goal **f**, which is in the process of being proved, the list of remaining choices is (2, 3, 4). This means that clauses 2, 3, and 4 of procedure **f** have not yet been executed to prove **f** at this precise point of the proof tree. Clauses 2, 3, and 4 are thus the choices that have not yet been considered by Prolog but that may be in the future.

Each call to a procedure has its own independent list of remaining choices. If a procedure is called several times, it is clear that the list of choices associated with each call is independent of the others.

In the example above

. goals **c** and **e** are already proved,
. goals **a**, **d** and **f** are in the process of being proved,
. goal **b** remains to be proved.

2. The Execution Process

Prolog has a procedural interpretation or, in other words, a strategy for the construction of proofs. This interpretation has been mainly defined in terms of an efficient memory space management. Other choices, more specific to certain applications, have been used in other languages less known than Prolog. The choice of a particular procedural interpretation has consequences for different facets of programming in Prolog.

Let us now examine the basic execution of a Prolog program. Two processes affect the progress of an execution:

(1) The normal progress of goals to be proved, where calls are executed in a sequential fashion, in the order in which the clauses appear in a program.
(2) Backtracking, which occurs either after a success in finding other solutions to a problem or after a failure to prove a goal. Backtracking is applied only to the preceding goal. Backtracking over several levels only occurs when there are no more possible choices at the intermediate levels.

At each call, the variables introduced by this call may be substituted by other variables or by functional terms. Note carefully that

(1) Two variables, initially free and different, may be bound together during a substitution.
(2) Once substituted by a term, a variable cannot be

substituted by another term, except when the variable is unbound from its value during backtracking.

If a variable is substituted by a term that itself contains free variables, these new free variables may, in turn, be affected by substitutions.

When backtracking occurs as the result of a failure to prove a goal, this means that there are no more possible choices at this point in the proof: the list of remaining choices is empty. The system then returns to the preceding choice and restores the state of the variables at this level. The next clause given by the list of choices for this instance of the call is then considered. If the list is empty, the system goes up to another level.

The analysis strategy of Prolog, for reasons of efficiency and economy of memory space, is thus the classic strategy of left-to-right, depth-first search.

To illustrate the resolution mechanisms, here is an example of the advancement of the resolution process, where unification causes the evolution of the form of the terms being manipulated. Consider the program

f :- g(X,Y), w(X,Z).

g(X,t(X,Y)) :- r(X).
r(u(a,b)).

Once **g** is called, the call to **f** will produce

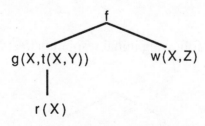

because **Y** is replaced by **t(X,Y)** during the unification. The variable **Y** in **t(X,Y)** is not the same as the **Y** in the call to **g** from the clause **f**. After the execution of **r**, we obtain

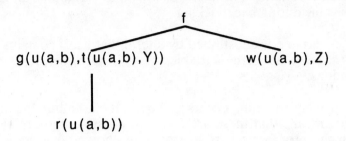

Using literals without arguments for simplicity, we now illustrate, with a very short example, the resolution strategy. We assume the following clauses:

a :- f.
a :- g.

b :- h.
b :- q.

and the facts

f .
g .
h .
q .

The call to prove is:

d :- a,b.

We have the following initial resolution tree:

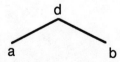

To prove **a**, we attempt to use rule **a :- f.** ; to prove **b**, we attempt to use rule **b :- h**:

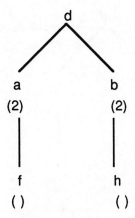

The list of choices is empty for **f** and **h** because they are ground facts and hence without alternatives. This constitutes a first proof.

Another case arises if we return to **b** (e.g., if **h** cannot be proved):

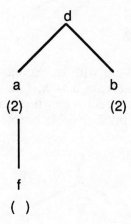

We can now try to prove **b :- q.** :

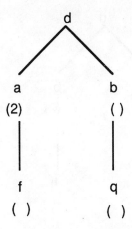

There are no more alternatives to **q**. This is a second possible proof. If there is a return to **b** (because of failure or to find another solution), then, since there are no more ways to prove **b**, it is necessary to return to **a**.

It is possible that another proof of **a** may have consequences that will allow us to prove **b**, when there are arguments.

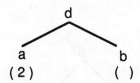

We try again to prove **a** with its second possible choice, the rule **a :- g.** and **b** with the rule **b :- h.** (we try the first choice again because it may be correct when there are arguments in the literals). We then obtain a third possible proof:

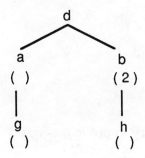

We then return to **b**, and there still remains one choice:

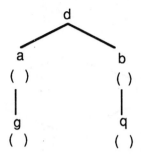

This is the fourth and last choice. If a failure occurs in all of these four choices, then **d** cannot be proved.

This set of proofs can be represented in a more concise manner by means of an AND-OR tree. This type of tree permits the representation of sets of elements that must all be proved (AND nodes) and of groups of elements of which only one must be proved to ensure the truth of the result (OR nodes).

AND nodes are represented as in the following example:

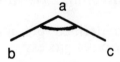

which means that to prove **a**, it is necessary to prove both **b** and **c**.

OR nodes are represented as in the following example:

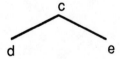

This means that **c** is true if either **d** or **e** is true.

In an AND-OR tree, the AND and OR nodes appear alternately. Two nodes of the same type may never follow each other.

The example given in this chapter resumes in the following manner:

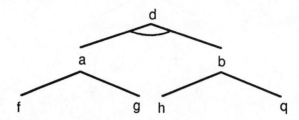

This AND-OR tree means that to prove **d**, one must prove both **a** and **b**, and to show **a**, one must show either **f** or **g**. Finally, to prove **b**, one has to prove either **h** or **q**.

This type of representation is very convenient for showing clearly the different possible ways of conducting a proof. The Prolog system scans the different branches in a depth-first order, beginning with the left branch as explained above.

3. Predicates for Controlling Resolution

There are two predefined predicates that permit the programmer to control the proof process:

(1) the predicate that provokes the failure of a proof and
(2) the predicate that allows the suppression of choices.

The predicate **fail** is always evaluated to true, and when it is executed, the value of the current clause becomes false. Thus, in the clause

a :- b, c, fail.

even if **a :- b,c** is evaluated to true, the execution of **fail** will produce false as a final result. If **b** or **c** is false, then **fail** is never executed; **a** is also false, but for a different reason.

The predefined predicate that suppresses the remaining choices (also called the *cut symbol*) is written **!** . This predicate is always evaluated to true, and when it is executed, it suppresses all of the possible remaining choices for all the literals going up to the head of the current clause, including that head predicate.

For example, suppose that we have, just before the execution of the cut, the following proof tree:

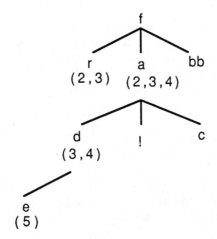

After execution of !, the state of resolution becomes

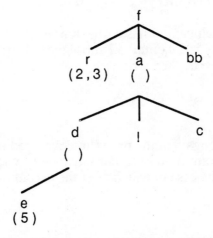

The control is then immediately passed on to **c**, and all backtracking from **c** goes directly to **f**, since the remaining choices on **d** and **a** have been eliminated by the cut. Consequently, the remaining choices on **e** will not be considered. The remaining choices at **r** can now be examined.

The cut symbol essentially allows the writing of efficient programs, by avoiding the necessity of searching through all possibilities when we wish to know only if at least one solution to a problem exists. It also permits a more convenient expression of *if A ...then B ...else C* constructs by not requiring the conditional to be written twice. In this case the *then* part (which follows the literal of the head of the first clause) contains the cut symbol. This is illustrated in Section 4, to write the negation.

The cut symbol must be used with extreme caution, as it can change the intended meaning of a program. Also, the use of the cut usually makes the order of clauses in a program very important. In spite of these restrictions, the use of the cut has undeniable advantages. These are illustrated in the five brief examples that follow:

(1) Our first example shows, for a very simple case, how to increase the efficiency of a program. Given the facts

```
country(france,  paris,  french).
country(spain,  madrid,  spanish).
country(italy,  rome,  italian).
```

and the rule

```
capital(X) :- country(_, X, _).
```

and knowing that each capital has a different name, once we have determined that a city is a capital, all subsequent searches have no further meaning. We may then write

```
capital(X) :- country(_, X, _), ! .
```

(2) Let us look again at the program developed in Chapter 7, Section 1. This program functions in a satisfactory way. However, if we wish to avoid the case in which after the execution of

```
number(X,10).
```

Prolog searches for a second solution that then leads to an infinite loop caused by the second clause, we can conveniently add a cut symbol:

```
number(X,10) :- ! .
number(X,E)  :- write(X),
                E1 is  E + 1,
                X1 is  X + 2,
                number(X1,E1).
```

Thus, once the first clause is executed, the second clause will not be executed again at this level of the proof.

(3) Now, let us take another look at the program given in Chapter 3, Section 2:

```
grandfather_of(X,Z) :-  child_of(Z,Y),
                        child_of(Y,X),
                        masc(X).
```

If we are simply interested in the existence of a grandfather **X** of **Z** and not in knowing wether **Z** has several grandfathers, we can introduce the cut at the end of the clause:

```
grandfather_of(X,Z) :-  child_of(Z,Y),
                        child_of(Y,X),
                        masc(X), ! .
```

Note that we cannot introduce the cut earlier in the clause, since if we do, we risk encountering a failure of a constraint that comes after the cut, when we have already excluded the possibility of examining other choices.

This could happen in the following clause:

```
grandfather_of(X,Z) :-  child_of(Y,Z),
                        child_of(Z,X), ! ,
                        masc(X).
```

where no backtracking is possible if **masc(X)** is not true with the current value of **X**.

(4) In Chapter 6 we gave a possible program for finding the maximum of two numbers:

```
max(X,Y,X) :- X >= Y.
max(X,Y,Y) :- Y > X.
```

Observe that, for any given execution, if the first clause's condition is false, then the second clause's condition is necessarily true. We can then write

```
max(X,Y,X) :- X >= Y, ! .
max(X,Y,Y).
```

This program says that, if **X** is greater than or equal to **Y**, then the result is **X** and the system does not need to consider the second clause of the program, which is suppressed. In the opposite case the result is **Y**.

This method is more efficient whatever the result: If **X** is the largest number, the Prolog system stops the search at the end of the first clause. If **Y** is the greatest number, the cut is not evaluated because the search is blocked by the condition **X >= Y** and there is no condition to evaluate in the second clause. Note the importance of placing the cut in the clause.

The order of the clauses is now very important. We may not permute them or else **Y** would always be the response because that clause has no attached conditions. For this reason the cut must be used with caution.

The introduction of the cut here has, however, modified the meaning of the program so that it now produces an erroneous result in certain cases. Indeed the call

    ?- max(5,3,3).

results in the response true when obviously the correct answer is false. The removal of the condition **Y > X** in the second clause is not totally compensated for by the introduction of the cut.

(5) Finally, consider the predicate **diff(X,Y)**, which returns true if **X** and **Y** are not unifiable. The program is written

    diff(X,X) :- ! , fail.
    diff(X,Y).

If there is a unification with the head of the first clause, the cut takes effect and the second clause will never be executed at this level of the proof. In the first clause the use of the same variable **X** in the two arguments forces them to be equal and therefore not different. The first clause terminates with **fail**, in order that, if the unification succeeds, the result will be false. The second clause is activated only if the first cannot be used, that is, if the two arguments of **diff** cannot be unified with the same constant. Thus, the call

    ?- diff(a,a).

will result in the answer false.

Note that the predicate **diff** presented here is local to the clause that calls it. That is, it responds with true or false according to the information contained in the clause that is currently calling it. In certain Prolog systems the **diff** predicate is predefined and guarantees that two uninstantiated arguments will never, throughout the entire proof, be equal. This is valuable when the clause contains only variables not yet bound to constant values.

This last example shows a necessary use of the cut, not merely for making the program more efficient, but rather for giving the program the desired meaning. Note again the extreme importance of the order of the clauses. The cut plays a major role here; we call it a *red cut* because it must be used with caution. Cuts used only to improve efficiency have no influence on the meaning of the program and are thus less problematic; they are called *green cuts*.

4. Negation as Failure

The predicate **not(P)** returns the value true if the predicate **P** is false and false if the predicate **P** is true. The program of **not** is written

not(P) :- P, !, fail.
not(P).

If the unification with the head of the first clause is a success, Prolog attempts to execute **P**. **P** must always be instantiated with a literal for an execution to be possible. If the result of the proof of **P** is true, the cut is involved. The second clause cannot now be executed, and the predicate **fail** causes Prolog to return false. If **P** is false, the first clause returns false. Then the second clause is executed; it returns true.

Note that the system is able to proceed to the second clause because it was not able to reach the cut in the first clause.

The program means that if **P** can be proved, the result is false (since **P** is true). Otherwise, the result is true (because it is not possible to prove **P**).

In some versions of Prolog, variables can appear only as arguments. Here, **P** is a term and constitutes a condition to be verified. For this reason **not** is very often a predefined predicate.

The use of negation increases Prolog's expressive power by authorizing negative conditions. It is now possible to use the equality symbol = to define **diff**:

diff(X,Y) :- not(X = Y).

which advantageously avoids the use of the cut. The clause is also easier to understand.

We have already used the relation **child_of(X,Y)**; now we can write the rule **without_child(Y)**, which is true if **Y** does not have any children:

without_child(Y) :- not child_of(_,Y).

Note that in the case in which **not** is predefined when it precedes a term, the use of parentheses is optional. The negation is applied only to the following term.

It is possible to use negation in questions:

?- not masc(marie).

Negation in Prolog is not exactly equivalent to negation in mathematical logic. If we ask the question

?- not masc(pierre).

and if Prolog responds

   yes

this means that there is not enough information in the knowledge base to prove that Pierre is of the masculine sex. If Prolog is not able to find the fact **masc(pierre)**, then the result is false and **not masc(pierre)** is true.

This mode of reasoning is tied to the closed-world assumption, which says that everything that cannot be proved from the current knowledge base is assumed to be false.

This mode of reasoning may appear far from the way humans process knowledge. It seems sufficient for the interrogation of simple databases. Beyond this type of application, however, it is preferable to envisage a multivalued logic that can be expressed in Prolog by creating a small interpreter on top of the Prolog system.

One may, for example, envisage a very simple system with three values, true, false, and unknown. In the fact base, we can then state the facts that are true and those that are false. The others will be assumed to be unknown rather than false. This idea is developed in Chapter 14.

It is advisable to be extremely cautious when variables in a term are in the scope of a negation. Consider the following base:

```
human(anne).
human(edith).
human(john).

animal(fido).
animal(rover).

masc(john).
masc(fido).
masc(rover).

fem(X) :- not masc(X).
```

If we ask the question

```
?- human(X), fem(X).
```

Prolog returns

```
X = anne;
X = edith.
```

Whereas if we ask the logically equivalent question

```
?- fem(X), human(X).
```

Prolog responds

```
no
```

In this case, **fem(X)** always fails because for all **X** extracted from **masc(_)** (here John, Fido or Rover), **fem(X)** is false.

In spite of these restrictions and precautions, cuts and

negations are very powerful and useful tools. It is indeed difficult to conceive of the development of complete applications without their use.

Exercises

Ex. 8.1

Write, using the definition of **diff(X,Y)**, the predicate **diff3(X,Y,Z)** that is true if **X**, **Y**, and **Z** are all different.

Ex. 8.2

Write a program that calculates the retail price from the wholesale price (retail price = wholesale price + profit), using the following conventions to calculate the profit:

> Price $\leq$ $100 : 20% profit,
> $100 < Price $\leq$ $1000 : 15% profit,
> Price > $1000 : 10% profit.

Ex. 8.3

Write the following rules:

(a) A large family has at least three children; use a call of the form **large_family(X)**, where **X** is a parent.

(b) Every person is a friend of John, except those who are friends of Martine.

(c) An animal is everything that is neither a human, an object, nor a plant.

Chapter 9

Lists

Lists are a data structure frequently used in Prolog. They permit us to model a large number of diverse problems. There are numerous simple programs associated with the list structure. These are useful in numerous applications and are presented here.

1. Representing Lists

Lists permit us to assemble sets of objects of any kind. The set

$E = \{ luke, edith, fido, roner, hildegarde \}$

can be represented in Prolog by the list

[luke,edith,fido,roner,hildegarde]

The opening bracket indicates the beginning of the list, and the closing bracket indicates its end. Elements of the list are separated by commas. This list can be represented in the form of a tree in the following manner :

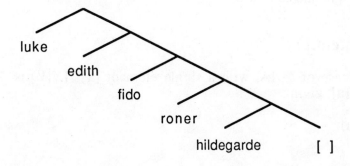

This tree is called a binary tree because each node has two daughters.

In comparison with a set, a list places a fixed and total order on its elements. The elements of a set may be permuted without changing the set, whereas it is not possible, in general, to permute two elements of a list without changing the list.

The first element of a list is called the *head* of the list, and the subsequent elements constitute the *tail* (or the body) of the list. In the example above **[luke]** is the head of the list, and the sublist **[edith,fido,roner,hildegarde]** is its tail. This process is recursive: the sublist **[edith,fido,roner,hildegarde]** itself has a head **[edith]** and a tail **[fido,roner,hildegarde]**. The empty list is written [ ]. The list **[blue]** has one element; in this case the head is blue and the tail is the empty list. A list of one element can indeed be noted: **[blue,[ ]]**.

Each element of a list is either a term or a list. The following list contains two terms and a list as elements:

[a(X,Y),[b,c,d,e],Z]

The list is a data structure that permits the representation of a group of very diverse objects. There need be no a priori relation between these objects. A list is a structure very different in nature and uses from facts and a tool for knowledge representation that complements facts.

In terms of unification, the essential list operation is the separation of the head and tail. This requires two variables: **X** for designating the head and **Y** for designating the tail. The symbol | is used to separate the head from the tail.

Consider the list **[a,b,c,d,e]**. It is unified with **[X|Y]**. **X** and **Y** are then bound as follows:

X = a
Y = [b,c,d,e]

In the case of a list with a single element **[a]**, **[X|Y]** is unified with **[a]**, giving

X = [a]
Y = [ ].

On the other hand, [X|Y] cannot be unified with the empty list [ ], since the empty list cannot be divided into two elements.

2. Searching for an Element in a List

There are a number of basic operations on lists that are useful in many applications. The main operations are given here; the others, less common, are given in the exercises.

The first operation consists of determining whether an element belongs to a list. The general principle is to scan the list, element by element, to see wether the desired element is present. More precisely, the method consists of comparing the head of the list with the element that is being sought. If there is a match, the result is true. If the desired element is not found at the head of the list, the system scans the sublist that remains after amputating the head. The process is repeated recursively. The search stops at the end of the list. If we write **found** each time the element is found in the list, the program can be written as

```
member_of(X,[X|_]) :-  write('found').
member_of(X,[_|Y]) :-  member_of(X,Y).
```

The first clause describes the case in which there is a match between the desired element (here, the first argument of **member_of**) and the head of the list. Whether or not the match succeeds at the head of the list, the program continues with Prolog invoking the second clause. This second clause causes the system to proceed through the rest of the list by extracting the sublist **Y** and calling **member_of** again. The program stops eventually when the current sublist cannot be unified with either [X|_] or [_|Y], that is, when the list is empty. The stopping condition is not stated explicitly.

To the call

```
?-  member_of(a,[e,f,a,f,h,i,a,a,c]).
```

Prolog will reply **'found'** three times. To stop the program as soon as one solution has been found, we can use the cut:

```
member_of(X,[X|_]) :- ! .
member_of(X,[_|Y]) :-  member_of(X,Y).
```

When the first clause is executed, the call to **member_of** is evaluated to true. The execution is then stopped because, after the cut is encountered, it is not possible to call the second clause, which contains the recursive call.

Note the use of [X|_] and [_|Y], where the underscores indicate that we are not interested in what is at the tail or head, respectively, of a list. This avoids useless unifications (see Chapter 4, Section 2).

3. Set Operations

It is possible to verify common set relations, such as inclusion, disjunction, and intersection, by using a list structure. We give several sample programs; other set relations may be written in a similar fashion.

Assume that we have sets **X** and **Y**, represented by two lists. The program **subset(X,Y)** returns true if all the elements of **X** also appear in **Y**. In order to deal with sets (represented as lists), we add that the elements of **X** can appear in any order in **Y**, since elements in a set are unordered. Because of this stipulation the question

   ?- subset([a,b,c],[e,a,c,d,b,g]).

will be evaluated as true.

The subset problem can be solved by considering the elements of **X** one by one and verifying that they appear in **Y**. The verification step is performed by calling **member_of**. The program stops when **X** is the empty list:

   subset([   ],Y).
   subset([X1|X2],Y) :- member_of(X1,Y),
                          subset(X2,Y).

As soon as an element of **X** does not belong to **Y**, **member_of** fails and **subset** is consequently evaluated to false.

The problem is slightly more complex if we wish to determine whether a sublist is included in a list. In this case it is necessary to find the entire sublist in the large list, in the correct order and without discontinuities. For example, **[a,b,c]** is included in **[e,a,b,c,d,f]** but not in **[e,b,c,d,a,f,t]**.

The program is similar to the previous one, but with a second level called **next**, which is activated when the beginning of the sublist is found in the list that is being scanned. The **next** clauses determine whether the entire sublist appears in the list. If not, the control returns to **sublist** through backtracking, and the state of the list before the call to **next** is automatically restored. This permits the scanning of the principal list to continue after this "false alarm." The program is the following:

```
sublist(Y,[ ]).
sublist([X1|X2],[X1|X3]) :- next(X2,X3).
sublist(X1,[_|X4]) :- sublist(X1,X4).
next([ ],Y) :- write('found').
next([X1|X2],[X1|X3]) :- next(X2,X3).
```

If **next** succeeds, the control is passed to **sublist**, which continues the search in the list with the immediately following element.

It is interesting to write a program that determines whether two lists are disjoint, that is, have no element in common. For example,

[a,b,c,d] and **[f,g,h,i]**

are two disjoint lists. To solve this problem, we make use of a very important property of Prolog clauses: the ability to instantiate or not to instantiate particular arguments of a clause. Depending on which arguments are instantiated, the answers may vary widely. We shall see in Chapter 17, which deals with the analysis of natural language, that it is possible to execute a program "in reverse" by supplying the result and letting Prolog deduce the data.

Consider again the progam **member_of(X,Y)** without the cut symbol. If **X** is free in a particular call, **member_of** permits the extraction, one by one, of all the elements of **Y**. When given the question

?- member_of(X,[a,b,c,d]).

Prolog will respond

X = a
X = b
X = c
X = d
yes

The program **disjoint(X,Y)** is then written

disjoint(X,Y) :- member_of(W,X),
                    member_of(W,Y),
                    !, fail.
disjoint(X,Y).

In general, the use of the sequence **!, fail** allows us to force a clause to fail when W is common to **X** and **Y**. This is the equivalent of writting a loop. Here, if **member_of(W,Y)** is true, we know that **X** and **Y** have an element W in common. The cut and failure then follow. If **member_of(W,Y)** is never evaluated as true, the first clause will never be completely executed. The second clause will then be evaluated to true.

The predefined predicate **repeat**, which exists in certain versions of Prolog, generates new branches in the proof tree for all the calls that follow it in a clause.

Another set operation is the computation of the cardinality of a set. The program is written recursively:

card([ ],0).
card([X1|X2],C) :- card(X2,C1),
                    C is C1 + 1.

The stopping condition, given in the first clause of the procedure, states that the length of the empty list is 0. The second clause of the procedure gives the recursive formula: the length of the list **[X1|X2]** is the length of the sublist **X2** plus 1.

In this example we use left recursion. There is no risk here of infinite loop because each time the procedure is called, the list to be examined is shorter.

Let us examine in detail what this program does. We consider the call

?- card([a,b],C).

The different levels of the execution of this call are described below. We first explain the recursive call and we examine what happens once the recursive calls are finished.

(1) Unification is only possible with

card([X1|X2],C)   :- card(X2,C1), C is C1 + 1.
X1 = a, X2 = [b],
recursive call: **card([b],C1).**

(2) Unification is possible with

card([X1|X2],C) :- card(X2,C1), C is C1 + 1.
X1 = b, X2 = [ ],
recursive call: **card([ ],C1).**

(3) Unification is possible with

card([ ], 0).

Second part: return to the calling progam:

Goal (3) is proved, so there is nothing more to do. For goal (2) the call to card is proved and it is known that C1 = 0, so the execution proceeds of

C is C1 + 1.
C = 0 + 1 = 1.

Goal (2) has been proved. For goal (1) the call to card is proved and it is known that C1=1, so the execution proceeds of

C is C1 + 1.
C = 1 + 1 = 2.

The final result is

C = 2.

4. Concatenation of Two Lists

Another very frequent operation is the concatenation of two lists. To concatenate means to juxtapose two lists to form a single list. Given the call

?- conc([a,b,c,],[d,e,f,g],Z).

Prolog will respond

Z = [a,b,c,d,e,f,g]

The general form of the predicate **conc** is

conc(X,Y,Z).

where **Z** is the concatenation of **X** and **Y**. The program is

conc([   ],Y,Y).
conc([X|Y],W,[X|T])   :-   conc(Y,W,T).

This program is composed of two clauses. The first clause says that the concatenation of the empty list with another list is the second list. The general case is more complex; to avoid producing sublists in the resulting list (**X** concatenated directly with **Y** would give a list composed of two elements: [[X],[Y]]), it is necessary to break apart the first list, element by element, and to reconstruct it inside the second list. This is expressed in the third argument. The number of recursive calls required is then solely a function of the size of the list in the first argument.

When **conc** is called, the value associated with **T** in the third argument ([X|T]) is calculated during the return from the recursive calls, since the value of **T** is unknown before this time. In fact, it is during the execution of

conc([ ],Y,Y).

that **T** is instantiated to the value of the second list. This result is relayed back to the recursive call immediately above by the variable **T**. The list [X|T] may then be determined, **X** being the head and **T** the tail. This process continues all the way back to the initial call, where the resulting list is displayed.

The program **conc** may be used for other purposes, depending on which arguments are instantiated. The call

?- conc(X,[d,e,f],[a,b,c,d,e,f]).

binds to **X** the beginning [a,b,c] of the list [a,b,c,d,e,f], of which the remaining part is found in **Y**, bound to [d,e,f].

Similarly, we may also ask

   ?- conc([a,b,c],Y,[a,b,c,d,e,f,g]).

In this case, the answer is the end of the list:

   Y = [d,e,f,g].

Finally, **conc** may be used to produce all the possible ways of breaking down a list into two lists. To the call

   ?- conc(X,Y,[a,b,c,d]).

Prolog will respond

X = [ ]	Y = [a,b,c,d];
X = [a]	Y = [b,c,d];
X = [a,b]	Y = [c,d];
X = [a,b,c]	Y = [d];
X = [a,b,c,d]	Y = [ ].

This example is a concrete illustration of how Prolog produces all the possible answers to a problem.

5. Palindromes

We have seen that there is only one method of accessing elements of a list in Prolog: by extracting the head and the tail of the list. The system always starts from the beginning of the list. This can be inefficient and burdensome to anyone interested in the last element(s) of a list.

A technique for facilitating the writing of programs is to reverse the list. For example,

[e,d,c,b,a] is the reverse of [a,b,c,d,e].

To reverse the list **X** and obtain the list **Y**, a recursive schema must be defined. The stopping condition states that the reverse of the empty list is this same list. The clause that contains the recursive schema can resolve the problem in a general way by stating that a list **X** is reversed by extracting the head of the list (**X1**), reversing the tail of the list (**Y** into **Y1**), and concatenating

Y1 with **X1**:

```
reverse([ ],[ ]).
reverse([X1|Y],R) :-  reverse(Y,Y1),
                      conc(Y1,[X1],R).
```

We can now define a palindrome by using **reverse.**

A palindrome is a word that reads exactly the same from right to left, or left to right. Examples are "radar" and "madam." To find out wether a word is a palindrome, we represent it by a list containing the characters in the word

```
[r,a,d,a,r]
[m,a,d,a,m]
```

We then apply **reverse** by stating that a palindrome is identical to its reverse:

palindrome(X) :- reverse(X,X).

This program handles words of any length, regardless of whether the number of letters is odd or even.

Exercises

Ex. 9.1

Write a program that counts the number of occurrences of a character in a list. The call will be

?- number_chars(X,C,N).

where, in more declarative terms, **N** is the number of occurrences of **C** in the list **X**.

Explain how this program can be used to select lists (given in the form of facts) that have exactly three occurrences of the character "a."

Ex. 9.2

Write a program that extracts the first **N** characters of a list and places them in another list.

Ex. 9.3

Write a program that extracts the last **N** characters of a list and places them in another list.

Ex. 9.4

Write a program that subtracts one list from another. Assume the call

?- subtract(X,Y,Z).

where **Z** is the subtraction of **X** from **Y**. Subtracting one list from another consists of removing all the elements of **X** that are in **Y**. For example, the result of subtracting **[a,b]** from **[e,a,c,b,g]** is **[e,c,g]**.

Ex. 9.5

Write a program that concatenates two lists **X** and **Y** and places the result in a list **Z** such that, if **X** and **Y** have common elements, these elements appear only once in the resulting list **Z**. Assume that **X** and **Y** taken separately do not contain any duplicate elements.

Ex. 9.6

What does this progam do?

```
m :- m1(X), write(X), nl.

m1(X) :- animal(Y),
         animal(Z),
         conc(A,B,Y),
         conc(B,C,Z),
         conc(Y,C,X).

animal([c,a,t]).
animal([t,u,r,t,l,e]).
animal([s,e,a,g,u,l,l]).
```

```
animal([l,e,o,p,a,r,d]).
animal([c,o,w]).
animal([h,o,r,s,e]).
animal([c,o,b,r,a]).
animal([r,a,b,b,i,t]).
animal([b,i,t,c,h]).
animal([g,u,i,n,e,a,f,o,w,l]).
animal([s,e,a,l]).
animal([a,l,l,i,g,a,t,o,r]).
animal([o,w,l]).
```

Chapter 10

Predefined Predicates

In the preceding chapters some predefined Prolog predicates, such as **not**, **write**, **!**, and **is**, were presented. In this chapter we present several other predefined predicates which will enable us to perform operations that were, up to this point, impossible.

These predicates allow us, among other things, to know what kinds of terms we are manipulating, to construct new terms inside a program, to test different types of inequalities between two terms, and to have more elegant input-output procedures.

Additional predefined predicates are presented in the chapter dedicated to deductive databases because they are more related to that area.

Definition and uses of predefined predicates depend in large part on the version of Prolog in use. All the predicates presented here are in very current use. Very similar ones can be found in almost all versions of Prolog. A complete list of predefined predicates for the syntax presented here is given in Appendix B.

1. Identifying Kinds of Terms

We have seen that a term may take many diverse forms: a variable, a constant, a number, an atom, or a predicate. The predefined predicates presented in this section allow us to test terms and to determine their types. This may be very useful before undertaking an operation. For example, it may be useful to know wether a particular term being manipulated is a free variable or is bound to a constant. For the operation

X is 3 ∗ 5.

it would be good to ensure beforehand that **X** is a free variable.

Here are the predefined predicates that allow us to identify a term's type:

var(X)

is true if **X** is a free variable.

nonvar(X)

is true if **X** is not a free variable.

atom(X)

is true if **X** is bound to an atomic value.

integer(X)

is true if **X** is bound to an integer number.

The following questions are evaluated as true:

```
?- var(X).
?- var(Z), Z = 'toto'.
?- integer(55).
?- X is 3 + 4, integer(X).
?- X is 3 + 4, nonvar(X).
?- atom(abc).
```

The following questions are evaluated as false:

```
?- integer(X).
?- Z =  'toto', integer(Z).
?- Z = 3/4, integer(Z).
?- Z = 3 - 4, var(Z).
?- atom(f(a,X)).
```

To illustrate the use of these predefined predicates, we shall develop a very simple example. Imagine that we have a rudimentary mailing system such that, when the user **U** has no message, the variable **M** that contains the message is free. At some given instant suppose that we have the database

message(john,[hello,from,jack]).

```
message(edith,[no,work,today]).
message(luke,M).
message(max,M).
```

John and Edith each have a message waiting, stored in the form of a list. Luke and Max do not have any waiting message. When the user queries the system for messages and when there is no message, the system then replies "no message at this time." Otherwise, the message is printed. The program is the following:

```
mailing(U) :-  message(U,M),
               var(M), !,
               write('no message at this time').
mailing(U) :-  message(U,M),
               print(M).


print([ ]).
print([M1|M2]) :-  write(M1),
                   write(' '),
                   print(M2).
```

If the call is, for example,

```
?- mailing(edith).
```

The response is

no work today.

Once the message is printed, it might be interesting to ask wether the user wishes the message to be saved. If the user wishes to save the message, there is nothing more to do. If he or she wishes to destroy the message, we must replace the list that contains the message with a variable. We do this by destroying the fact and adding a new one in which the *message* argument contains a variable.

We present this technique here in an informal way and in a more general fashion in the chapter on deductive databases.

2. Decomposition and Construction of Terms

The predefined predicate for the decomposition and

reconstruction of terms is written

X =.. Y

where **X** is a term and **Y** is a list. This predicate breaks a term
down into a list:

?- f(X,a,b,c) =.. Y.
Y = [f,X,a,b,c]

or makes a term out of a list:

?- X =.. [f,X,Y,t(2,K)].
X = f(X,Y,t(2,K))

This predefined predicate has many uses, which are illustrated in
the chapters dedicated to applications.

For now, let us reconsider the example of the preceding
section. Suppose that, as before, when a message is read, it may
then be destroyed at the request of the user. One possible way to do
this is to transform the corresponding fact **message(U,M)** into a
list, to replace the message **M** by a variable **M1**, and to recreate the
fact. This new fact can then be added to the beginning of the list of
facts in the mailing system. The old fact will not be consulted again
because of the use of the cuts. It would, in fact, be interesting not
actually to destroy a message so that we could also construct a
message history.

To carry out the program, we need the predefined predicate
asserta(F), which is equivalent to **assert(F)** (see Chapter 1)
except that it places the fact **F** at the head of the list of facts named
F.

We shall also need the predefined predicate **read(X)**, which
reads an atom and puts it into variable **X**. The program is written

```
mailing(U) :- message(U,M),
              var(M), !,
              write('no message at this time').
mailing(U) :- message(U,M), !,
              print(M),
              cancel(U,M).

print([ ]).
print([M1,M2]) :- write(M1),
```

```
                              write(' '),
                              print(M2).

cancel(U,M) :-  write('do you wish to destroy the
                   message?'),
                   read(Response),
                   Response = yes, !,
                   message(U,M) =.. Mess,
                   modify(Mess,Mess1),
                   New =.. Mess1,
                   asserta(New).
cancel(U,M).

modify([message,U,M],[message,U,M1]).
```

Note that the second clause in the procedure **cancel(U,M)** is always evaluated to true. It is only executed when the user does not respond **yes**, because of the cut in the first clause of the procedure. When the response of the user is negative, nothing needs to be done.

To complement this predicate, which decomposes and reconstructs terms, two other predefined predicates permit access either to the name of a predicate (this name is also called a functor) or to a particular argument.

The predicate

functor(T,F,A)

extracts the name **F** from the term **T**. Argument **A** gives the arity of the term **T**, that is, the number of arguments it possesses. To the call

        ?- **functor(f(1,g(X,Y),H),F,A).**

Prolog responds

        F = f
        A = 3

The predicate **arg(N,T,A)** extracts argument number **N** from the term **T**. The extracted argument is placed in **A**. To the call

        ?- **arg(2,f(h(1,2),g(a,b,c,d),P,X),A).**

Prolog responds

    A = g(a,b,c,d).

These two predicates can be defined in terms of the predicate that decomposes and reconstructs terms. This is shown below for the predicate **functor1**, simplified because we do not give the arity (which is equal to the length of the list **Z** below minus 1).

    functor1(T,F) :- T =.. Z,
                  extract(Z,1,F).

The predicate call **extract(Z,1,F)** extracts the element in position 1 in **Z** and places it in **F**. The program for extract is given below.

Predicate **arg** is defined completely as follows:

    arg(N,T,A) :- T =.. Z,
             extract(Z,N+1,A).

    extract([Z1|Z2],1,Z1).
    extract([Z1|Z2],N,Z3) :- N is N - 1,
                extract(Z2,N1,Z3).

3. Input-Output Operations

Input-output operations remain relatively rudimentary in most versions of Prolog. So, users must define for themselves any more complex operation they desire to use.

We have already presented three basic input-output operations:

write(X)   write the contents of **X**,

nl   skip to the following line,

read(X)   read an atom and place it in **X**.

It is necessary to terminate an element to be read with a period so that Prolog knows when to stop reading.

In standard versions, more complex predicates that, for example, place spaces between elements or limit the number of decimal places in a number, do not exist. There is only the predicate

tab(N).

which leaves **N** spaces before the next item is printed.

Some predefined predicates for file manipulation do exist. These files must always be sequential. The user terminal is treated as if it were an ordinary file, with the name "user." These predicates direct the system's attention from the current file to file **F**:

see(F)   the file **F** becomes the new input file,

tell(F)   **F** becomes the output file,

seen   closes the current input file,

told   closes the current output file.

An example of the use of these predicates is given in Chapter 16, Section 6.

4. Defining New Operators

It is possible to define new Prolog operators (sometimes called *directives*) inside a program. A new operator must be defined before it is used by means of the predefined predicate **op**, for example,

:- op(400,xfy,d7).

Note that the predicate is preceded by :-, which, when the program is interpreted, causes the system to execute the definition as if it were a question posed by the user. The definition contains three parts:

(1) **400** is a number that indicates the priority we wish to attribute to the newly defined operator. This priority is relative to that of the already existing operators. The priorities of the common operators are defined in the system (the higher the number, the greater the priority) and are shown below:

:- , ?-	1200
logical operators	700
+ , -	500
* , / , div	400
mod	300

The priority of a newly defined operator must be less than 1000, which is the priority of the comma.

(2) **xfy** indicates the type of the operator **f**. In this case there is an operand (**x**) before and an operand (**y**) after the operator. When the operands have a lower priority than that of **f**, **f** is written **xfx**. If the priority of the argument is greater than that of **f**, it is written **xfy**.

It is also possible to define *prefix* operators **fx** (such as **not**) or *postfix* operators **xf**.

(3) **d7** is the name of the operator and can be any constant. We can now write, for example,

   6 d7 48+7

This says that **6** and **48+7** are related by relation **d7.**

An operator defined in this way does not allow us to perform operations on data. It is used to build structures, exactly like a fact. In some cases these operators prove very useful and are more elegant than ordinary facts. This is the case when defining new programming languages on top of Prolog.

It is possible to define as many operators as one wishes in a Prolog program. To conclude, here is a short example of an operator use:

Given the operator **is,**

   :- op(800,xfy,is).

and the data

   john is a painter.
   luke is a musician.
   edith is a scientist.

we can use questions of the type

?- **edith is X.**

to which Prolog responds

X = a scientist.

The use of defined operators may be especially appreciated by noncomputing users who wish to define data items without having to create Prolog facts.

It is sufficient in these cases to define operators such as **is,** **possesses,** and **gives.** The definition of new operators is well suited to syntactic analysis where the symbol **-->** is commonly used. An example of this use is developed in Chapter 17.

Exercises

Ex. 10.1

Write the program **write1(X),** where **X** is a list composed either of variables or of integer numbers. **write1** prints the contents of the variables and leaves a number of spaces equal to numbers given in the list. For example, to the call

?- **write1([X,2,Y,7]).**

Prolog will write the contents of **X** followed by two spaces, followed by the contents of **Y** and then seven spaces. Add a control that signals an error if, as above, the last element of the list is a number (thus asking Prolog to print spaces).

Chapter 11

Some Programming Advice

Prolog allows concepts to be expressed at a relatively high level of abstraction compared with the usual programming languages. The syntax is simple and a lot of freedom is given to the programmer. Prolog programs are often shorter than their procedural equivalents. The high abstract level of Prolog permits the development of applications in a relatively short time.

The programmer, however, must be careful not to neglect certain principles of well-designed programming. We briefly review these principles in this chapter.

The method of analyzing problems and programming their solutions differs from those used with classical approaches, so the programmer must enter a new mode of thinking. This mode can only be acquired after writing several programs in a somewhat rigorous manner. It is extremely difficult to propose a methodology for programming in Prolog; we provide here some advice and the rudiments of a method that we have found to be well adapted.

1. General Principles

A program must be *readable* and *clear* . This means it must be well presented and sufficiently well spaced. The procedures must not be too long and therefore difficult to understand, nor, should they contain too many arguments. It is also advisable to limit the use of the symbol ; for regrouping the clauses of simple programs, so as not to compromise readability.

A program must be *modular*: a complex problem must be broken down into subproblems, which can then be handled independently. The subproblems are then integrated into more general procedures that essentially express constraints and relate the arguments of different calls to subproblems.

A program requires a main call to manage the subproblems. It is possible to have several levels of decomposition, and Prolog is well suited for the modular expression of problems. The programmer is also advised to create a library of short and frequently used programs so as not to have to rewrite them for each application.

A program must be *robust*. This means that in the case of an error, in data entry, for example, it must not stop abruptly but rather have a helpful attitude toward the user. In particular, it is essential to check data.

In the case of a negative response to a user's question, it is also useful for the program to indicate, in the form of a brief message, why the response is negative.

A program must be *well annotated,* but without useless comments. This is particularly crucial for Prolog, where it is not an easy task to read the clauses. It is always advisable to explain the meaning of each argument of the head of the clause and then to explain briefly what the clause does.

The absence of global variables in Prolog allows a more complete and autonomous comment for each clause or procedure.

There are two methods of inserting commentaries in a program: A long commentary must begin with /* and end with */ . When it is sufficient to write a few words at the end of a line after a call, the beginning of the comment is indicated by the symbol % . In this case the end of the line indicates the end of the comment. Here is an example:

/* calculate the average of two numbers, X and Y are the two numbers and R is the result of the calculation */

```
average2(X,Y,R) :- Z is X + Y,
                    % sum of the two numbers.
                    R is Z/2.
                    % divide by two.
```

Finally, a program must be *efficient*. There are several techniques for achieving this, which are specified in Chapter 11, Section 4. Note that some very efficient Prolog systems now exist; the time has passed when execution times are measured in hours or days.

2. Top-Down Approach

One possible method of programming in Prolog is to analyze the problem, first in a global fashion and then to refine each aspect.

First of all, it is useful to specify the main aspects of the problem and the different steps that will be required to solve it. This confers a certain degree of modularity to the program.

Once the different aspects of the problem have been distinctly identified, they should be ordered in sequence.

The next step is to decompose each aspect of the problem into subproblems in the same manner. This is called a *top-down* approach.

Once the problems to be solved become sufficiently simple, it is possible to proceed to the programming stage. During this stage the programmer must maintain a grasp on the overall problem, as well as on its subproblems.

This makes it possible to identify common problems that appear in different places and to write clauses that are sufficiently general to be used during the programming of different subproblems.

Never hesitate to generalize the different cases handled by clauses in order to make them more widely applicable. Generalization often leads to greater programming ease and, in many cases, greater readability. Generalizations must not, on the other hand, be excessive, or they may cause a noticeable decline in the overall efficiency of the program.

Formal grammars and the rewriting systems allow problems to be modeled in an efficient, modular, and top-down manner. Moreover, it is possible to define extensions to Prolog that allow direct conversion of such modes of representation into Prolog programs. Thus, programs become more transparent.

We shall see a brief example in Chapter 17, dedicated to the analysis of natural language. Because of their high level of abstraction, it is suggested that formal grammars and rewriting systems be used by experienced programmers.

3. Testing Prolog Programs

Testing of a Prolog program begins with the consideration of the clauses at the lowest level, those that perform the simplest tasks with a minimum of calls to other clauses.

It is possible to test these clauses by calling them directly from the user interface of the Prolog system and giving them diverse values that are appropriate to their arguments. In Prolog every clause may be called and executed independently of the main program: an important advantage over many other programming languages.

When these clauses work correctly, the clauses at the next level up can be tested. These next clauses usually contain calls to the clauses that have just been verified. The process goes on in this manner up to the main clause.

A Prolog programmer has many different techniques available for finding and solving problems: intermediate results can be viewed by using the predefined predicate **write** or by tracing the program. The predefined predicate **trace** allows the programmer to visualize the different steps of an execution. This predicate may be used in two ways. If **trace** is called before starting the execution of a program, Prolog displays line by line the trace of the execution. The user may interrupt the execution at any time with the command **a** for **abort**:

```
?- trace.
yes
?-  call to a program.
traces........
.........?   a
```
Prolog execution aborted

A call to **trace** can also be inserted directly into the program at the precise spot at which the problem exists. To stop the tracing of the program, insert the call **notrace** at the point at which tracing is no longer desired:

```
a(X,Y,_) :-  b(X),
             trace,
             c(X,_),
             g(f(Y)),
             notrace,
             h(Y,X,_).
```

The trace does not explicitly show all the execution steps; it gives more information about the branches of the proof that have ended in a success or that appear to be following a successful path. Each line of the trace contains indications of the type **fail** or **back to**.

4. Thinking in Prolog

In the preceding chapters we have attempted to give some major principles for programming in Prolog. These have included the declarative mode and the expression of constraints.

Prolog permits the expression of knowledge in *"declarative mode."* This means that the data are stated without concern for the manner in which they will later be executed.

A Prolog program consists of a series of relatively independent statements. This approach permits improved clarity and reliability and thus allows a greater ease of modification.

It is also possible to express knowledge in *"procedural mode,"* that is, in the same way as in a classical language. Prolog was not initially conceived with this mode in mind, but it may prove useful in many cases, particularly for defining a loop without the use of recursion. Some problems can be implemented more simply and naturally without recursion, by using loops.

Recursion remains, however, a major form of expression in Prolog. The principle is always the same: A phenomenon is described at an arbitrary level N as a function of the results obtained at the preceding level $N - 1$. A stopping condition, placed at the head of the procedure, ensures the termination of the process. The recursion process is initialized during the call to the recursive clause by appropriate instantiation of arguments.

Prolog is well adapted to classes of problems that manipulate objects and the relationships between these objects. It is important to define which relations are best suited to the problems to be solved, with adequately structured arguments. Well-structured data greatly facilitate the writing of a program by limiting the number of clauses and augmenting their efficiency.

Finally, a judicious use of cuts limits the size of the solution search tree and improves efficiency. When cuts are used to increase efficiency, in general, they barely affect the readability of the program.

The storing of facts with the predicate **assert** causes the system to remember solutions that it has already worked out and avoids searching for the solution to a problem many times. Assertions must always be used carefully, however, for in many systems the available memory space is not completely recoverable and there is a risk of overflowing the memory.

We recommend that the programmer adopt a style of programming that is as close as possible to the declarative mode. In this mode it is more easily seen that the program is correct. However, the programmer must also keep in mind Prolog's method of executing clauses, not only to ensure the efficiency of the program but also to ensure that, when the program is executed, it will actually perform what the programmer intended. These two aspects may seem somewhat contradictory, but experience shows that good Prolog programming contains an appropriate and sometimes subtle balance of both of these aspects.

5. Toward Applications

This advice cannot be assimilated simply by reading it. Effective programming in Prolog demands long practice, which can be reduced somewhat by considering the advice given here.

Programming in Prolog is illustrated in the following chapters, which present games and simple applications of artificial intelligence. Certain limitations of Prolog are also presented, as well as means of creating extensions to the language.

Whether Prolog can be used for developing industrial applications is still the subject of debate. There are at least two reasons for this. Prolog is a young language some of whose definitions still need to be refined. It also still lacks a good programming environment. However, much effort has been successfully invested in developing efficient compilers and interpreters.

The other reason is that Prolog is not always used for the purposes for which it was conceived. An appropriate use of Prolog in eventual collaboration with other programming languages for handling certain problems would seem to be a rewarding strategy. This raises the problem of interfacing Prolog with other programming languages.

In other respects, Prolog, by its very nature, lends itself to the definition of extensions. The idea is to define a language, preferably a simple one, on top of Prolog. The language would be defined for a particular type of application and would simplify the programming of this application. The language could be interpreted in Prolog so that the programs written in it could be translated automatically into Prolog. A very simple example, developed in Chapter 17, concerns string manipulations when writing grammars.

Finally, an important element in the realization of an application is its transportability. It is therefore expedient, before developing any very specific implementation, to keep in mind the degree of transportability that might be required.

Chapter 12

Formal Aspects of Programming in Logic

Prolog is the main language of the logic programming paradigm. The goal of this chapter is to clarify the relationships between Prolog and mathematical logic, as well as to state more formally its declarative and procedural semantics. The reading of this chapter is important, although not necessary for an understanding of the chapters that follow. A number of the ideas given in this chapter have already been introduced intuitively in the preceding chapters. This chapter is not overly concerned with formalisms; the reader is referred to more detailed works given in the Bibliography.

In this chapter we give the definition of *first-order logic* (hereafter referred to as *FOL*), then of *clausal forms* and *Horn clauses*. The major aspects of declarative semantics of Prolog procedures are then examined, and Prolog's basic mechanism of resolution (*SLD resolution*) is clarified. The chapter ends with some remarks about the meaning of a Prolog program.

1. First-Order Logic

First-order logic (FOL), as all languages in general, consists of two complementary aspects: syntax and semantics. Syntax characterizes the forms of expression and formulas of a language. Semantics assigns a meaning to the symbols employed in these formulas.

We now define the syntax of FOL. FOL is composed of constants, predicates, and function symbols. A predicate p of arity n is composed of a predicate symbol followed by n terms: $p(t_1, t_2, ..., t_n)$. The same is true of a function f of arity m: $f(t_1, t_2, ..., t_m)$. A term is a constant, a variable, or a function of arity m:

$f(t_1, t_2, ..., t_m)$, where every t_i is a term. A well-formed formula of FOL is traditionally defined in a recursive way, as follows:

(1) $p(t_1, t_2, ..., t_n)$ is a formula (or an atom because of its elementary form) if p is a predicate of arity n and if every t_i is a term.

(2) if A and B are formulas, then so are

$\neg A$ (negation of A)

$A \wedge B$ (A and B)

$A \vee B$ (A nonexclusive or B)

$A \Rightarrow B$ (A implies B)

$A \Leftrightarrow B$ (A is equivalent to B)

(3) if X is a variable and A a formula, then

$((\forall X)A)$ (A is true for all values of X)

and

$((\exists X)A)$ (there exist some X for which A is true)

are formulas of FOL.

Parentheses may be used whenever there is a risk of ambiguity.

There is a meaning associated with each of the operators introduced above ($\neg$, $\wedge$, $\vee$, $\Rightarrow$, $\Leftrightarrow$). A simple way to give the meaning of a symbol is to use a *truth table*, which gives the truth conditions of a formula using that symbol. For example, to give the semantics of $\neg$, we have the following truth table:

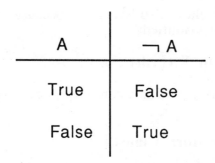

A	$\neg$ A
True	False
False	True

For the symbol $\vee$, **A** $\vee$ **B** is true if either **A** or **B** is true; **A** $\wedge$ **B** is true if both **A** and **B** are true; **A** $\Rightarrow$ **B** is true if, whenever **A** is true (respectively, false), **B** is true (respectively, false); **B** may also be true when **A** is not:

A	B	A => B
True	True	True
True	False	False
False	True	True
False	False	True

Finally, **A** $\Longleftrightarrow$ **B** is true when **A** and **B** are either both true or both false.

In $((\forall X) A)$, the formula **A** is in the scope of the quantifier $(\forall X)$, and **X** is bound to this quantifier.

A closed formula is a formula where all the variables appear in the scope of a quantifier. Thus, for example, the following formula is closed:

$$((\forall X)h(X,t(a,b)) \wedge f(4,7))$$

whereas the following formula is not closed because **X** is not quantified:

$$(f(4,X) \wedge ((\exists Y)h(Y,t(a,b))))$$

The following formula is also not closed because only the second occurrence of **X** is quantified:

$(f(4,X) \wedge ((\forall X)h(X,t(a,b))))$

In the rest of this chapter we only consider closed formulas.

2. Clausal Forms and Horn Clauses

Most actual automatic proof techniques are based on a restricted form of FOL. Prolog itself is based on one of the most restricted clausal forms, *Horn clauses,* so that the required calculations can be efficiently performed on a computer. A clause is a formula of the following form:

$$\forall X_1, X_2, ..., X_n \ (A_1 \vee A_2 \vee ... \vee A_p)$$

where each A_i is an atom or the negation of an atom (here called a literal) and $X_1, X_2, ..., X_n$ is a set of variables that appear in the disjunction

$$(A_1 \vee A_2 \vee ... \vee A_p).$$

Here are two examples of formulas that are clauses:

$$\forall X,Y(f(X,2) \vee g(h,Y,7) \vee \neg p(X))$$

$$\forall X(\neg p(X)).$$

The following formula:

$$\forall X, \ Y \ (f(X,2) \wedge \neg g(h,Y,7))$$

is not a clause because it uses the logical AND ($\wedge$).

In logic programming, it is the tradition to group together the literals that precede the negation; this does not change the meaning of the clause because OR is a commutative operation. The formula (a) becomes (b):

$$\forall X_1, X_2, ..., X_n,$$
$$(A_1 \vee A_2 \vee ... \vee A_n \vee \neg B_1 \vee \neg B_2 \vee ... \vee \neg B_m)$$

with $p = n + m$ and the same conditions as above. This formula is logically equivalent to (c):

$$\forall X_1, X_2, ..., X_n((A_1 \lor A_2 \lor ... \lor A_n)$$
$$<= (B_1 \land B_2 \land ... \land B_m))$$

because $(\neg B_1 \lor \neg B_2)$ is equivalent to $\neg(B_1 \land B_2)$ and $(B_1 \Rightarrow B_2)$ is equivalent to $(\neg B_1 \lor B_2)$. This can be verified with the help of truth tables.

$(B_1 \land B_2 \land ... \land B_m)$ is called the *antecedent* of the implication and $(A_1 \lor ... \lor A_n)$ is the *consequent*. The B_i's are sometimes called *negative literals* and the A_i's *positive literals*.

This leads us to a definition of *Horn clauses*. A Horn clause has one of the following forms:

(1) $\forall (X_1, X_2, ..., X_n)$ $(A <= B_1 \land B_2 \land ... \land B_m)$
(2) $\forall (X_1, X_2, ..., X_n)$ $(A <=)$
(3) $\forall (X_1, X_2, ..., X_n)$ $(<= B_1 \land B_2 \land ... \land B_m)$

Intuitively, form (1) corresponds to a Prolog rule where **A** is the head and $B_1 \land B_2 \land ... \land B_m$ is the body. Form (2) is a fact, possibly containing some variables. Finally, form (3) corresponds to a question (or goal) in Prolog. Forms (2) and (3) are particular cases in which the body or the head (respectively) of the clause is empty.

Forms (1) and (2) are universally quantified, as they are implicitly when a Prolog program is written. The domain of possible values for each variable is always limited to the domain of constants given in the program at the moment the execution takes place. A rule can thus be read:

for all assignments of values to $X_1, X_2, ..., X_n$, if $B_1 \land B_2 \land ... \land B_m$ is true, then **A** is true.

Form (3), which corresponds to a question in Prolog, requires additional explanation. We have seen that such a clause may be put into the form

(4) $(\forall X_1, X_2, ..., X_n)$ $B_1 \land B_2 \land ... \land B_m \Rightarrow \square$.

This clause, which implies an empty result (denoted $\square$), expresses a contradiction. It gives the conditions under which $B_1 \land B_2 \land ... \land B_m$ is false. This approach is called a *refutation*; it will be developed in the following sections. Formula (4) above is equivalent to

$$(5) \quad \forall X_1, X_2, ..., X_n \ (\neg B_1 \vee \neg B_2 \vee ... \vee \neg B_m)$$

and also to

$$(6) \quad \neg \exists \ X_1, X_2, ...,X_n \ (B_1 \wedge B_2 \wedge ... \wedge B_m)$$

The negation of this expression:

$$(7) \quad \exists \ X_1, X_2, ..., X_n \ (B_1 \wedge B_2 \wedge ... \wedge B_m)$$

then characterizes situations where $(B_1 \wedge B_2 \wedge ... \wedge B_m)$ is true. This is the underlying form of a question in Prolog. Each B_i is a subgoal to be proved.

3. Declarative and Procedural Semantics of Prolog

Prolog is composed of two aspects, logic (Horn clauses) on one hand and control on the other. The logical aspect expresses the problem to be solved and how solutions can be found, apart from any computational preoccupation. The control part states precisely how a proof can be mechanically carried out. Ideally, these two parts should be independent and complementary. In the preceding chapters we have seen that this is unfortunately not the case. There are some important divergences that make the writing of programs and, more generally, the elaboration of a methodology for programming in Prolog very delicate (see Chapter 11).

For now, we consider Prolog to be a set of facts and rules, as well as goals (or questions) to be proved. The declarative semantics of Prolog is based on that of Horn clauses. More precisely, let us consider a program **P** and a goal **B** to be proved. The proof technique by *refutation* consists of showing that **P** and $\neg$**B** result in a contradiction:

$$P \wedge \neg B \Rightarrow \square .$$

and thus that **B** must be true since **P**, the program, is by convention a set of true axioms. In particular, we obtain the values of variables $X_1, X_2, ..., X_n$ found in **B** for which **B** is true. The declarative semantics of Prolog is, therefore, that a goal **B** is deduced from a program **P** if $P \wedge \neg B$ cannot be proved.

The procedural semantics of Prolog appears to be a specification of its declarative semantics with the automation of the mechanism of proof by refutation. The proof strategy that has been adopted is that of top down, depth first, and left to right. This strategy is associated with the mechanism of resolution and, in particular, SLD resolution. This is discussed in the following section.

4. SLD Resolution

The fundamental principle of SLD resolution is a method of rewriting modulo substitutions. A goal of the form

$$B_1 \wedge B_2 \wedge ... \wedge B_i \wedge ... \wedge B_m \Rightarrow \square.$$

associated with the clause

$$C_1 \wedge C_2 \wedge ... \wedge C_p \Leftrightarrow B'_i.$$

with θ being the minimum set of substitutions such that $B_i\theta = B'_i\theta$ is rewritten as

$$[B_1 \wedge B_2 \wedge ... B_{i-1} \wedge C_1 \wedge C_2 \wedge ... \wedge C_p \wedge B_{i+1} \wedge ... \wedge B_m] \theta \Rightarrow \square.$$

This is called the *resolvant* of the goal and of the previously given clause.

The rewriting process presented here is called goal reduction. This process is applied a finite number of times to the original goal **B** (the question posed).

The termination condition applies either when the resolvant is empty (**B** is proved) or when it is no longer possible to apply the rewriting techniques (in which case **B** is false). The general schema of SLD resolution given above shows a resolvant that is longer than the goal. In fact, reductions often appear with facts (which have an empty body). This is illustrated below; from the goal: $B_1 \wedge B_2 \wedge B_3 \wedge ... \wedge B_n \Rightarrow \square.$ and the fact $B'_2 <=.$, modulo the substitution θ_2, we obtain

$$[B_1 \wedge B_3 \wedge ... \wedge B_n] \theta_2 \Rightarrow \square.$$

The mechanism of SLD resolution that we have just described is derived directly from the inference rule of *modus ponens* . Replacing the head of a rule by its body or removing facts from a goal comes from the fact that in a program the rules and the facts play the roles of axioms.

5. SLD Resolution in Prolog

The mechanism of SLD resolution allows for many automatic implementations; the choice of which goals to reduce and which clauses to use remains to be specified. The choices are specified through a calculation rule (or strategy) **R** associated with SLD resolution. The rule **R** has no fundamental influence over the result. However, depending on the rule **R**, the size of the proof tree (and thus the global efficiency of the system) may be very different. Some difficulties may also appear with recursion.

In the example that follows, two calculation rules are considered:

R_1: The reduction of subgoals in a goal proceeds from left to right.

R_2: The reduction of subgoals in a goal proceeds from right to left.

Consider the program **path(X,Y)** given in Chapter 7, Section 2, which gives true as a result if there is a path from **X** to **Y**:

```
(1)  path(X,Y)  :-  arc(X,Y).
(2)  path(X,Y)  :-  arc(X,Z),  path(Z,Y).
(3)  arc(a,b).
(4)  arc(b,c).
(5)  arc(c,d).
```

The use of the calculation rule R_1 gives the following proof tree, where branches are labeled with the rule number and the substitutions are used to apply the rule:

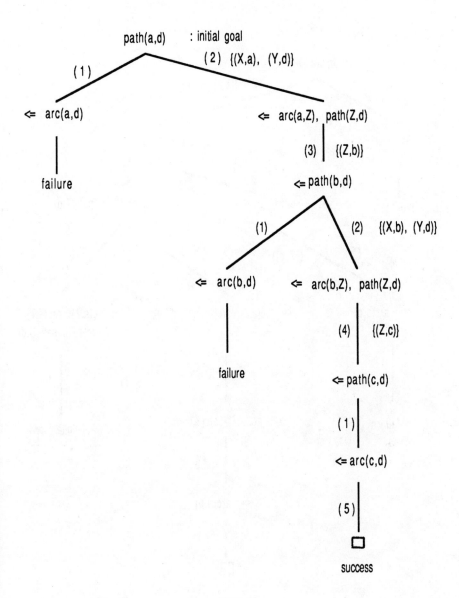

With calculation rule $\mathbf{R_2}$, the following proof tree is obtained:

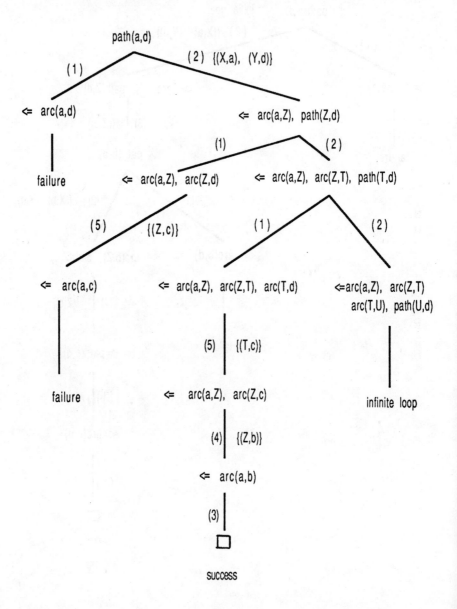

The path that results in success is longer with R_2. Moreover, the program enters into an infinite loop in the last branch of the proof tree. Prolog uses calculation rule R_1, which reduces subgoals from left to right.

Numerous deep problems are, however, uncovered by making this choice, which was motivated by computing considerations that the reader may find in the specialized works cited in the bibliography.

6. Meaning of a Program

From a formal point of view, the meaning of a program is the set of elementary completely instantiated goals that can be deduced from the program. This set may be infinite, particularly when recursive definitions are used.

The meaning of a program must coincide with the meaning the programmer wishes to express. If this requirement is difficult to meet, it is advisable at least that the meaning of a program be contained within the meaning the programmer wishes to confer on it. Ideally, the meaning of a program should be independent of the underlying automatic proof mechanism. In reality, because of the compromises that were made, in particular, those to make the system efficient, this independence is not attained. Programming in Prolog is therefore a delicate task. Nevertheless, Prolog's properties make it very attractive for numerous applications, the basic aspects of which are developed in the following chapters.

Chapter 13

Playing with Words

This chapter describes various well-known games that can be solved in interesting ways in Prolog. We solve the game of crisscross and then generalize it to the automatic fabrication of crossword puzzles (without definitions!). Next, we present a small game of dominos (number or word based) and finally, the game of finding the longest word given a set of letters.

The goal of this chapter is to familiarize the reader with the techniques for handling lists. Diverse techniques for analyzing problems are proposed and discussed.

1. Crisscross Puzzles

Given a list of words (called a *dictionary*) in the form of facts and a grid such as the one shown below, the problem is to place the words of the dictionary in the grid, taking into account the intersections. Here is an example of a grid:

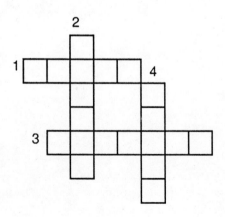

Here is the same grid filled with arbitrary words:

The problem consists of stating that the third character of the first word, which has five letters, is equal to the second character of the second word, which has six letters, and that the fifth letter of the second word is the same as the second letter of the third word, which has seven letters, and so on.

There are at least two ways of expressing this problem. We could decompose it into subproblems to facilitate writing it out, or we could express it in a purely declarative manner, in a single clause. The second way could be motivated by the fact that the problem is not very complex. The first approach is more methodical, so we shall present it first and in greater detail.

It is possible to break the problem down into very simple subproblems. A first task is to find words of the correct length in the dictionary, which is a set of facts called **word**. In our example we need words of length 5, 6, 7, and 5. We find these words here with the aid of clause **long**. Procedure **num_lets** counts the number of letters in a word. We must next extract the Nth letter of a word; we can do this with the clause **extract**. Finally, we need to compare two letters from two words and express the requirement that they must be the same. This is done with the clause **intersect**. The main call **crisscross** describes the structure of the grid.

Here is the program that solves this problem. Notice the manner in which we have decomposed the problem into subproblems. This gives us a simple modular program.

First, here is our dictionary of words:

```
word([m,a,r,k,e,t]).
word([t,r,e,e,s]).
word([m,o,n,k,e,y]).
word([s,i,m,p,l,e]).
word([w,i,s,e]).
word([v,a,g,u,e]).
word([s,e,a]).
word([y,a,c,h,t]).
word([o,c,e,a,n]).
word([f,o,g,g,y]).
word([a,r,t,i,s,t]).
word([r,e,a,l,i,z,e]).
word([b,r,a,v,e]).
word([q,u,i,t,e]).
```

/* Predicate **num_lets(T,X1)** is true if **T** is the number of letters in the word **X1**. */

```
num_lets(0,[]).
num_lets(T,[M1|M2]) :-  num_lets(T1,M2),
                        T is T1 + 1.
```

/* Predicate **long(T,M)** is true if **M** has length **T**. */

```
long(T,M) :-  word(M), num_lets(T,M).
```

/* Predicate **intersect(C1,C2,N1,N2)** extracts the letters in position **N1** from the list **C1** and the one in position **N2** from the list **C2**. It then asks whether the two extracted letters are the same. This is expressed through the occurrence of the same variable **R** in both calls to extract. */

```
intersect(C1,C2,N1,N2) :-  extract(C1,N1,R),
                           extract(C2,N2,R).
```

/* Predicate **extract(C,N,R)** is true if **R** is the Nth letter in the list **C** of letters. */

```
extract([C1|C2],  1,  C1).
```

```
extract([C1|C2], N, R) :- M is N - 1,
                          extract(C2,M,R).
```

/* Predicate **crisscross** is the main call. It selects words of the appropriate length for a given grid. The length of the words here is, respectively, 5, 6, 7, and 5. It places constraints on the words through predicate **intersect**. */

```
crisscross(M1,M2,M3,M4)  :-
                long(5,M1),   long(6,M2),
                    intersect(M1,M2,3,2),
                long(7,M3),
                    intersect(M2,M3,5,2),
                long(5,M4),
                    intersect(M3,M4,5,3).
```

For reasons of efficiency, it is important to use the **intersect** constraint as early as possible to limit the number of possible solutions and, in this way, to avoid some useless backtracking.

The **crisscross** program can also be written in a more compact, but less readable way, as follows:

```
crisscross([M11,M12,M13,M14,M15],
           [M21,M13,M23,M24,M25,M26],
           [M31,M25,M33,M34,M35,M36,M37],
           [M41,M42,M35,M44,M45])  :-

    word([M11,M12,M13,M14,M15]),
    word([M21,M13,M23,M24,M25,M26]),
    word([M31,M25,M33,M34,M35,M36,M37]),
    word([M41,M42,M35,M44,M45]).
```

You can try other grid configurations by varying the arguments to **intersect** in the first solution. You can generalize the program to create crosswords automatically. This will require a voluminous dictionary to provide a large number of word intersections. Describe only small grids; otherwise the execution time could approach a full day on a microcomputer!

Consider, for example, the following grid:

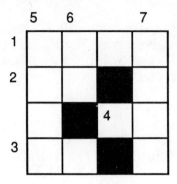

It can be described as follows:

crossword(M1,M2,M3,M4,M5,M6,M7) :-
    long(4,M1),
    long(2,M2),
    long(2,M3),
    long(2,M4),
    long(4,M5),
        intersect(M1,M5,1,1),
        intersect(M2,M5,1,2),
        intersect(M3,M5,1,4);
    long(2,M6),
        intersect(M1,M6,2,1),
        intersect(M2,M6,2,2),
    long(4,M7),
        intersect(M1,M7,4,1),
        intersect(M4,M7,2,3).

We leave it to the reader to write the program that prints the crossword grid.

2. The Game of Domino

Dominos is a game that manipulates numbers but that can also be transposed to words. The game is simple: It consists of juxtaposing sequences of dominos such that the neighboring parts of two dominos have the same numbers. For example, the sequence of dominos below is correct:

| 1 | 3 | | 3 | 6 | | 6 | 2 | | 2 | 5 |

Representing a domino is very simple: we define a fact **domino(A,B)** where **A** and **B** each represents half of a domino. Suppose that we have the following dominos:

```
domino(1,2).
domino(2,3).
domino(1,5).
domino(2,5).
domino(5,3).
domino(3,4).
domino(3,2).
domino(4,5).
```

/* To begin, a domino is selected. Then **sequence(L,B)** is called. **L** contains a list of the dominos already used. */

```
start :- domino(A,B),
         sequence([domino(A,B)], B).

sequence(L,C) :- domino(C,D),
                 not member_of(domino(C,D),L),
                 conc(L,[domino(C,D)], Z1),
                 sequence(Z1,D).
sequence(L,_) :- write(L).
```

The program stops either when it is impossible to add any more dominos to the sequence, or when all of the dominos have been used. Predicates **member_of** and **conc** are defined in the preceding chapters.

This program can be generalized to simulate a game between two players. Two sets of dominos must be defined, one for John, for example, and the other for Edith. The call **start(X,Y,A,B)** introduces the two players **X** and **Y**. Player **X** begins the game. **A** and **B** represent the two values of the first domino played by **X**. The alternation of plays is controlled by the recursive call to **sequence**. The program follows:

```
start(X,Y,A,B) :-
        domino(X,A,B),
```

```
                    sequence(Y,X,  [domino(X,A,B)],  B).
sequence(X,Y,Z,C)  :-
            domino(X,C,D),
            not member_of(domino(X,C,D), Z),
            conc(Z,  [domino(X,C,D)],  Z1),
            sequence(Y,X,Z1,D).    % switch players
sequence(_,_,Z,_) :- write(Z).
```

/* The fact **domino(X,A,B)** indicates that **X** has the
domino **(A,B)**. */

```
domino(john,1,2).
domino(john,3,4).
domino(john,5,1).
domino(john,6,3).
domino(edith,2,3).
domino(edith,1,5).
domino(edith,4,6).
domino(edith,3,1).
```

This program prints out a game of dominos. It is more
interesting, however, to know whether John or Edith wins! The
winner of the game is the one who can use the most dominos. This
can be formalized as follows:

(1) If **X** starts and ends the game, then **X** wins.
(2) If **X** starts the game and **Y** finishes, then if **Y** can play at
least one more domino after the one he has just played to end the
game, **Y** wins.
(3) Otherwise, the game is tied.

To implement this, we must modify the last clause of the
procedure **sequence** and add the definition of procedure
determine_winner:

```
sequence(X,Y,Z,C)  :-
            reverse(Z,Z1),
            determine_winner(X,Y,Z,Z1,C).

determine_winner(X,_,_,[domino(X,_,_)|_], _)  :-
            !, write(X),
            write(' has won the game.').
determine_winner(_,Y,Z,_,C)  :-
            domino(Y,C,D),
            not member_of(domino(Y,C,D), Z), !,
```

```
        write(Y), write(' has won the game.').
determine_winner(_,_,_,_,_) :-
        write(' The two players are tied.').
```

3. The Longest Word

This game consists of finding the longest word that can be formed from a set of letters given in any order at all. The idea is to combine these letters to form the longest word that you know.

It is necessary first of all to enter a dictionary so that the system knows vocabulary. To make the game interesting, the dictionary should be large.

Given a list of letters, we shall first find the set of words in the dictionary that can be formed from these letters. This is done quite easily by the procedure **in**, which looks at each word in the dictionary in turn to see wether it can be formed from the given letters. Letters must not be reused. To ensure that they are not, each time a letter in the word being considered is found in the list of letters, this letter is removed from the list. The process then continues with the letters remaining in the list.

The clause **form_words** ensures that every word in the list is checked. It contains a call to the dictionary followed by a call to **in** to see wether the word is eligible to be the longest word. If the call to **in** fails, backtracking causes **form_words** to choose another word from the dictionary. If the word is eligible, it is written down and the search continues.

To aid us in writing the rest of the program, we add facts labeled **word_found** to the fact base before printing the word. The program is written:

/* The longest word */

```
word([p,l,a,n,e]).
word([t,r,e,e]).
word([t,h,e]).
word([a,n]).
word([a]).
```

```
word([a,t,t,i,c]).
word([u,s]).
word([t,o]).
word([t,o,n,e]).
word([t,o,n]).
```

/* Verify that the word **M** can be formed from the letters in the list. */

```
in([M1|M2], L) :- remove(M1,L,L1),
                  in(M2,L1).
in([ ],L).
```

/* Remove the letters that match letter **M1** from the list **L**. Place the result in list **L1**. */ (see also Chapter 9, Section 4).

```
remove(M1,L,L1) :-
             decompose(L,L2,[M1],L3),
             conc(L2,L3,L1).
```

/* Main call: in the form of a loop. */

```
form_words(L) :- word(M),
                 in(M,L),
                 assert(word_found(M)),
                 write(M),
                 fail.
form_words(L).
```

/* Decompose list **M** into three sublists. */

```
decompose(M,M1,M2,M3) :- conc(M5,M3,M),
                         conc(M1,M2,M5).
```

If we now want to select the longest word, we must count the number of letters in each word and keep the longest against which to measure other words. The first step is to find all the words that can be formed out of the letters, as described above.

In the program we have presented, the words obtained were added as facts with the use of the **assert** predicate. Note the use of the **fail** predicate, which has allowed us to produce the set of words that could be formed out of the given letters before constructing the set of them. If **fail** is not used, as soon as one solution is found, the proof continues in the main clause, and consequently, we do not have available the full set of words to search for the longest one.

The call to the program that finds the longest word is **longest**:

```
longest(L) :- form_word(L),
              set_of(X,word_found(X),M1),
              longer(M1,M2,long),
              nl,
              write('The longest word is   '),
              write(M2).
```

/* This procedure finds the longest word. The first argument contains the list of words, the second the longest word, and the third the length. */

```
longer([ ],[ ],0).
longer([M1|M2],M1,L) :-  long(M1,L),
                         longer(M2,M3,L2),
                         L >= L2.
longer([M1|M2],M3,L2) :-  long(M1,L),
                          longer(M2,M3,L2),
                          L2 > L.
```

/* Calculate the length of a word. */

```
long([A|B],L) :- long(B,L,1), L is L1 + 1.
long([ ],0).
```

Infinite variations on this program can be made by adding constraints on the forms of words. The progam that plays this game can be made more efficient, for example, by using predicate **decompose**. Note, however, the declarative aspect of the program as written. The type of decomposition illustrated here makes it easy for us to add finer constraints at a large number of places in the program. Notice that, instead of using the assertion of facts and a call to **set_of**, we could have used an additional argument in **form_word** to store words.

The game presented in this section can also be solved in a completely different way, by combining different numbers of letters in all possible ways and verifying for each word whether it is in the dictionary. This seems to be less efficient, especially when the dictionary is small. This technique, called *generate and test* in classical programming, is of sufficient interest in Prolog for us to introduce it.

The principle consists of generating a word and then determining whether it will appear in the lexicon. To do this, the list **L** is decomposed into two sublists **M1** and **M2**; then **perm** generates all possible permutations **M3** out of **M1**. At the beginning of the execution of **conc**, **M1** is the longest list, but it diminishes in size as **M2** grows. This means that the first word **M3** for which **word(M3)** is true is the longest word. The program follows:

> **form_word(L)** :- **conc(M1,M2,L),**
> **perm(M1,M3),**
> **word(M3),**
> **write('the longest word is: '),**
> **write(M3).**

The definition of **perm(M,M1)** is as follows:

> **perm(L,[H|T])** :- **conc(V,[H|U],L),**
> **conc(V,U,W),**
> **perm(W,T).**
> **perm([ ],[ ]).**

The principle is to select an arbitrary element (**H**) and to place it at the head of the list, while producing permutations of the rest of the list.

Chapter 14

Deductive Databases

Prolog lends itself naturally to the specification and creation of databases. In fact, it offers additional facilities to those found in classic database systems, in particular, the ability to make deductions. This is why a Prolog database is called a *deductive database*.

Prolog offers a unified framework for representing data in a database, for formulating requests or questions, and for defining "views" and integrity constraints. A database can therefore be completely represented in Prolog. The facts or assertions constitute the *extensional* component (the completely instantiated data) and the rules form the *intensional* component.

With the development of efficient Prolog systems, deductive databases will undoubtedly supplant the relational database model in the relatively near future.

1. Basic Structures

A deductive database is composed of facts and rules. Rules are used for two purposes: to express additional knowledge, deductible from existing facts, and to control the knowledge and its evolution. In the latter case these rules are called *integrity constraints*. They are developed in the fourth section of this chapter. For now, let us simply say that rules allow us to deduce new knowledge from facts when the integrity constraints do not prevent us from doing so.

2. A Film Database

In this section a simple example with diverse kinds of queries is presented. Additional tools presented in the following sections will allow us to formulate more complex queries.

We now create and query a database of films that contains various kinds of information about films in three types of facts:

(1) film(title, year, director, genre).
(2) actor(last_name, first_name, sex).
(3) star(film_title, actor, role).

Here is the database from which we shall work:

film(bambi,41,disney,animation).
film(a_passage_to_india,84,lean,drama).
film(gone_with_the_wind,39,fleming,melodrama).
film(star_wars,77,lucas,science_fiction).
film(the_sound_of_music,65,wise,musical).
film(the_ten_commandments,56,demille,epic).
film(ben_hur,59,wyler,epic).
film(jaws,75,spielberg,suspense).
film(the_godfather,72,coppola,gangster).
film(return_of_the_jedi,83,markquand,science_fiction).
film(around_the_world_in_80_days,56,anderson,adventure).
film(doctor_zhivago,65,lean,romance).
film(grease,78,kleiser,musical).
film(saturday_night_fever,77,badham,musical).
film(raiders_of_the_lost_ark,81,spielberg,adventure).

actor(allen,woody,m).
actor(hamill,mark,m).
actor(ford,harrison,m).
actor(andrews,julie,f).
actor(plummer,christopher,m).
actor(gable,clark,m).
actor(leigh,vivian,f).
actor(heston,charleton,m).
actor(dreyfuss,richard,m).
actor(fisher,carrie,f).
actor(niven,david,m).
actor(travolta,john,m).
actor(newton_john,olivia,f).

star(around_the_world_in_80_days,niven,traveler).
star(the_sound_of_music,andrews,governess).
star(the_ten_commandments,heston,moses).
star(ben_hur,heston,ben_hur).
star(star_wars,hamill,luke_skywalker).
star(star_wars,ford,pilot).
star(return_of_the_jedi,hamill,luke_skywalker).
star(return_of_the_jedi,ford,pilot).

star(grease,newton_john,teenager).
star(grease,travolta,teenager).
star(saturday_night_fever,travolta,dancer).
star(the_sound_of_music,plummer,father).
star(raiders_of_the_lost_ark,ford,archaeologist).
star(gone_with_the_wind,gable,opportunist).
star(gone_with_the_wind,leigh,southern_belle).

We now write the following questions in Prolog:

(1) List the first and last names of the actresses.
(2) List the first and last names of the stars of the film "Gone with the Wind."
(3) List the first and last names of the stars, along with whom they have starred in at least one film.
(4) List the names of films that have no star.
(5) List the names of the stars who have only appeared in films directed by Kleiser.
(6) List the names of directors who have made at least two films.

We now show how these questions are written in Prolog. To make it easier to print the results, we define the following predicate, which prints a string followed by a blank space:

writeb(X) :- write(X), write(' ').

To make the sample queries more concrete, we show several possible responses after each prolog query. Remember that the questions are answered according to the data in the database ,which are not complete.

Question 1:

?- actor(X1,X2,f), writeb(X2), write(X1), nl.

julie andrews
vivian leigh
carrie fisher
olivia newton_john

Question 2:

?- star(gone_with_the_wind,X1,_),
actor(X1,X2,_), writeb(X2), write(X1), nl.

clark gable
vivian leigh

Question 3:

?- actor(X1,X2,_),   star(X3,X1,_),
film(X3,_,X4,_),   writeb(X2),   write(X1),
writeb(':'),   write(X4),   nl.

mark hamill: lucas
harrison ford: lucas
harrison ford: markquand
julie andrews: wise
etc.

Question 4:

We must use negation to avoid the films that have any stars as
actors.

?- film(X1,_,_,_),   not star(X1,_,_),   write(X1),
nl.

bambi
a_passage_to_india
jaws
the_godfather
doctor_zhivago

Question 5:

A way to answer this question is first to define the predicate
other_star. This predicate is evaluated to true when star X1 has
acted in at least one film not directed by director X2.

other_star(X1,X2) :-   film(X3,_,X5,_),
                         diff(X2,X5),
                         star(X3,X1,_).

The Prolog question is then written

?- film(X1,_,kleiser,_),   star(X1,X5,_),
not other_star(X5,kleiser),   write(X5),   nl.

newton_john

Note: To avoid printing the same name twice, we can keep track of actors whose names have already been found, for example, by adding new facts to the database.

Question 6:

?- film(X1,_,X3,_), film(X6,_,X3,_),
diff(X1,X6), write(X3), nl.

lean
spielberg

These questions have been formulated in Prolog in a somewhat rudimentary way. We now introduce some supplementary operations that will allow us to formulate questions that are more elegant, viable, and efficient.

3. Basic Operations

Just as with a relational database, the evolution of a deductive database is characterized by data modifications.

The first operation is the addition of facts. This is done with the help of the predefined predicate

assert(Fact).

This predicate adds the fact given in the argument to the end of the procedure with the corresponding name. Thus, we may add the following fact to the preceding database:

?- assert(film(annie_hall,81,allen,comedy)).

At the logical level, this fact will be added automatically to the end of the **film** facts. This predicate may also be used to add new rules during the execution of a program.

If we wish to add a fact to the beginning of the procedure, it is convenient to use the predefined predicate

asserta(Fact).

This is used in the same way as **assert**. In some versions of Prolog it is also possible to specify the position in the procedure at which a new fact is to be inserted.

The next operation is the deletion of a fact. This is accomplished with the aid of the predefined predicate

retract(Fact(...)).

The first fact in the database that is unified with **Fact(...)** is removed from the database. To delete, for example, the film "Jaws" from the database, the following call is used:

?- retract(film(jaws,_,_,_)).

If we want to delete all the facts in a procedure at once, we use the following predefined predicate:

abolish(N,A).

where **N** designates the name of the fact and **A** its arity. For example, to destroy all the **star** facts, we use the call

?- abolish(star,3).

The addition and then destruction of facts can be very useful for creating temporary facts. For example, we might wish to reuse some results that we have previously worked out and thereby avoid calculating them several times. When the execution terminates, all the temporary facts must be removed. An example of this strategy is given in the chapter on expert systems.

The last operation is the modification of the value of an argument of a fact. The existing fact in the database must be deleted, while still being retained by the program that is modifying it. The program modifies the argument, then adds the modified fact to the database. The modified fact will not occupy the same place in the database, but this generally does not matter. The most widely used versions of Prolog contain no predefined predicate of this kind. We therefore propose the following predicate:

modifarg(Fact,Arg_number,New_value).

Argument **Fact** designates the fact to be modified, given in its entirety, including arguments. **Arg_number** designates the number of the argument of the fact that is to be modified. **New_value** is the new value that is to replace the old value. To modify the genre of the film "Star Wars" from science fiction to space western, we create the call

?- modifarg(film(star_wars,77,lucas,science_fiction), 4, space_western).

The corresponding fact is destroyed, and its replacement is added to the end of the film procedure. The predicate **modifarg** can be implemented in the following way:

```
modifarg(X,Arg_number,New_value)  :-
        retract(X),
        X =.. Y,
        replace(Y,Arg_number+1,New_value,Z),
        Y1 =.. Z,
        assert(Y1).
```

/* In predicate **replace**, **Z** designates the new list, after the argument has been modified. In the second clause of **replace**, **Z** is reconstructed in the same way as in the program **conc**. */

```
replace([Y1|Y2],1,N,Z)  :-  !,  conc([N],Y2,Z).

replace([Y1|Y2],Arg_number,N,[Y1|Z1])  :-
        Arg_number1 is Arg_number-1,
        replace(Y2,Arg_number1,N,Z1).
```

4. Advanced Tools

The tools presented here allow us to query the database in a more complete way. We explain how to construct a set, sort data, and calculate an average value.

When there are several solutions to a problem, it might be useful to group them together in a list. It is then possible to do some calculations using this list, for example, to count the number of solutions.

The predefined predicate

```
setof(X,P,S).
```

creates the set **S** of all values of **X** that satisfy **P(X)**. **S** has the form of a list. For example, to find the set of names of people who are parents of children, we write

```
?-  setof(Y,child_of(X,Y),S).
```

We obtain

```
S  =  [john,edith,luke,max,martine]
```

When the second argument of the predicate **setof** contains several variables, it must be clearly specified which variable the set will be constructed from. In the example above, where we want to obtain a list of parents, we place **Y** in the first argument of **setof** instead of **X**, which would give the list of children. The variables used in **setof** are local to this predicate and, except for **S**, may not appear outside it. In most versions of Prolog the predicate **setof** ensures that only one instance of a particular solution is stored in set **S**. If we want to keep all the duplicates, predicate **bagof**, also called **listof**, is used instead:

```
bagof(X,P,S).
```

This may be useful, for example, to count the number of times a particular procedure was called, when some of the results may be identical.

Here is a simple implementation of **setof**, which we call **our_setof** to avoid any confusion The predicate **our_setof** makes use of assertions and retractions. We construct the list of those **X**'s that satisfy the property **P** (P can stand for a set of predicates, appropriately parenthesized).

The program is the following:

```
our_setof(X, P, S)   :-  asserta(find([ ])),
                         our_setof1(X,P,S).

our_setof1(X, P ,S) :-  P,
                        find(Z),
                        not member_of(X,Z),
                        retract(find(Z)),
                        conc(Z,[X],T),
                        asserta(find(T)),
                        fail.
```

```
our_setof1(X, P ,S) :- find(S), !,
                       retract(find(Z)).
```

The **our_setof** clause initiates the search by announcing that no element has already been found. It does this by adding fact **find([ ]))**, which will later serve to store the chosen elements. In the first clause of the procedure **our_setof1**, the facts that satisfy **P** are stored in the order of their discovery in the fact **find(X)**. This fact is recreated upon the discovery of each new fact. The use of **fail** at the end of the clause allows us to process all the facts by forcing Prolog to backtrack. The second clause of the procedure is the terminating clause. Set **S** is extracted from fact **find(X)**, and **X** is made equal to **S**. Notice that the call

not member_of(X,Z)

in the first clause permits us to eliminate duplicates (in addition to an infinite loop).

This implementation of **setof** is not very efficient However, it does show how this predefined predicate can be created, as well as showing the major difficulties and how they can be remedied. To conclude with the predicate **setof**, let us mention how it can be used to express negation:

not(P(X)) :- setof(X,P(X),[]).

In database systems, sorting operations are of primary interest. Many versions of Prolog contain one or more predefined predicates that perform sorts. The simplest predefined predicate is

sort(L1,L2).

which sorts the list **L1** in increasing order and places the result in **L2**. Duplicate elements are ignored. This predicate is fairly greedy in terms of memory space but is relatively efficient (its complexity is of the order of $n * \log(n)$).

Sorting is not very easy to program in Prolog, and there is an abundance of literature on the subject. Keeping in mind the introductory nature of this book, we present here only a "naive" sorting program, which is not efficient but very simple. The technique used is to permute the list and check each new result to see wether the list is sorted. The following program sorts a list in decreasing order:

```
sort(L,T) :-  perm(L,T),
              check(T).

check([A]).
check([A,B|C]) :-  A>=B,
                   check([B|C]).
```

5. Expressing Integrity Constraints

Integrity constraints take the form of rules and are used to control the evolution (addition, modification, and destruction) of data. Consider the following database, which contains two different kinds of facts about the employees of a company:

```
age(name,age_in_years).
employee(name,number,age,seniority,
         number_of_children).
```

The database is the following:

```
age(john,18).
age(anne,50).
age(cathy,25).
age(luke,44).
age(edith,32).
employee(john,1200,18,2,1).
employee(anne,1201,50,32,3).
employee(cathy,1202,25,6,0).
employee(luke,1203,44,17,2).
```

To control the evolution of these data, we may wish, for example, to ensure that the age of an employee never exceeds 80 years. At the same time, the number of years of seniority cannot be less than the number of children if we decide that each child automatically gives the employee an additional year of seniority. Finally, the number of years of seniority cannot be greater than the age of the worker. In Prolog, one possible way to express integrity constraints of the types described above is to state that a fact can be added to a database only if no contradiction is detected. This can be done as follows:

```
addfact(X) :-  coherent(X), assert(X).
        % Age is less than 81 years.
coherent(age(Name,Age)) :-  Age < 81.
        % There is no other worker with the same ID.
```

```
coherent(employee(_,ID,_,_,_)) :-
        not employee(_,ID,_,_,_).
coherent(employee(_,_,_,Number_of_years,Number_of
_children)) :-
        Number_of_years >= Number_of_children.
coherent(employee(_,_,Age,Number_of_years,_)) :-
        Age > Number_of_years.
```

More complex constraints do exist, and they require us to make use of times, sums, or averages of values to take into account several different kinds of facts, and so on. Although more complex, these constraints can generally be expressed in a fashion similar to those presented above.

6. Problems of Quantification

A major problem with the querying of databases is the processing of quantification. As a matter of fact, although it is simple to respond to a question that is expressed in existential terms (does such a fact exist and with what values?), it is much more complex to respond to questions that contain, in their English paraphrase, articles of the type

all of, many of, several, a majority, at least four, etc.

These articles raise numerous theoretical and concrete problems, among them, how to represent imprecision or fuzziness, and how to determine the scope of the quantification. These problems are mentioned here, the majority of them still remaining the subjects of active research in the areas of logic, linguistics, and artificial intelligence.

To show the truth of the proposition *for all values of X, P(X) is true,* where $P(X)$ is any property of X, it is sufficient to show that there exists no X such that $\neg P(X)$ is true. It can be deduced from this that $P(X)$ is true for all values of X. This is translated into Prolog by using negation and the negation-as-failure deduction rule.

To process an article such as *for a majority of X, P(X) is true,* it is necessary to evaluate all of the database elements that might potentially satisfy $P(X)$ and then verify that the number of elements that effectively satisfy $P(X)$ is indeed greater than the number that satisfy $\neg P(X)$. It is possible and more efficient to use a statistical sampling technique when the amount of data is very large. However, these techniques are not readily available in Prolog.

Articles, such as *many of, several of,* and *few of,* require a comparison of the same type as that used by *a majority of,* with the additional problem of interpreting the imprecision of these articles. In particular, the comparison criterion may not be simply *more than half,* but a measure that is highly context dependent, if it can be found at all. Some aspects of this problem can be handled in a better fashion by nonclassical logics such as default logic.

7. A World with Three Truth Values

Up to now, the application presented has implicitly used the *closed-world assumption*: every fact that cannot be proved in a finite time is assumed to be false. This method of reasoning is efficient and well adapted to simple objective situations. However, it soon proves to be approximate and naive for problems that are somewhat more complex. Many-valued logics, among other possibilities, allow us to alleviate a few of these insufficiencies. Since our goal is to make the reader aware of some of the problems surrounding Prolog, we shall limit ourselves here to bare outlines. In this section we present a system that uses a three-valued logic.

We can still use the closed-world assumption, but we use a different way of reasoning by distinguishing three categories of data: those we know to be true, those we know to be false, and finally, those about which we know nothing. We therefore attribute to these types of data the truth values: true, false, and undetermined, respectively. We have now introduced a three-valued logic.

We can now come to the problem of representing knowledge according to this system. One possibility is to represent explicitly the information that is known to be true and that which is known to be false and to mention nothing about data whose truth value is undetermined. In the database we must then distinguish the data that are true from those that are false. A simple and classic solution consists of adding an argument to each fact to indicate whether the fact is true (argument = 1) or false (argument = 0). Thus, if we know that *Max is Lucy's child* is true, we write

child_of(max,lucy,1).

Similarly, if we know that *Luke is Edith's child* is false, we write

child_of(luke,edith,0).

Or more generally, we can assert that Edith has no children as follows:

child_of(X,edith,0).

This kind of notation is mainly motivated by the need to make explicit only the information, either true or false, that is of immediate interest for the considered application.

Prolog is not able to process a system of three-valued logic directly. It is therefore necessary to write a program that interprets this system and makes it executable in Prolog. In particular, we must redefine the logical operators. We now show how to redefine the negation operator, which we call **not3** to avoid confusion with the classical negation operator. **not3** has two arguments: the second argument contains the truth value of the fact contained in the first argument, after the negation is applied. The value 0.5 is arbitrarily assigned to mean undetermined.

/* If the fact is true, its negation is false. If the fact is false, its negation is true. */

```
not3(P,V) :-  P,
              P =.. X,
              reverse(X,Y),
              value(Y,V),  !.

value([1|_],0).
value([0|_],1).
```


/* The negation of an undetermined fact is undetermined. */

```
not3(P,0.5).
```


Here is an example of a call using **not3**:

```
?- not3(child_of(lucy,catherine,X),Y).
```

The call to **P** in **not3** allows us to find the value of **X**. The fact **P** is then transformed into a list and reversed, as a way of providing rapid access to the last argument, no matter how many arguments the fact has.

We now examine how to handle the conjunction of two elementary questions. Given two facts **A** and **B**, the problem is to find the truth value of **A** AND **B**. We must first of all define the truth table for **A** AND **B**:

A	B	A and B
1	1	1
1	0	0
1	0.5	0.5
0	1	0
0	0	0
0	0.5	0
0.5	1	0.5
0.5	0	0
0.5	0.5	0.5

A simple rule can be used to summarize this truth table: The true value of **A** AND **B** is equal to the minimum truth values of **A** and of **B**. Here is the program that calculates the truth of **A** AND **B**, where **A** and **B** are two elementary goals. The call is

   ?- and3([A,B],V).

where **V** holds the result of the evaluation.

   /* **R A** and **R B** are the truth values of **A** and of **B**, respectively. **result** calculates the truth value of **A** AND **B**, and the final result is placed in **V**. */

```
and3([A,B],V) :-   prove(A,RA),
                   prove(B,RB),
                   result(RA,RB,V),
                   write(V).
```

```
prove(X,Y) :- X, !,
               X =.. L,
               reverse(L,[Y|Z]).
prove(X,0.5).

result(X,Y,X) :- X =< Y, !.
result(X,Y,Y).
```

It is simple to generalize this program in a recursive fashion to make it find the truth value of the conjunction of any number of predicates.

We can also similarly redefine the logical OR (**or3**): the value of **B** OR **A** is the maximum of the values of **A** and **B**.

By defining **not3, and3**, and **or3** to be operators in Prolog, we have at our disposal a simple language. Each formula of this language can be analyzed and assigned a truth value by using the programs given above.

The system of the three-valued logic that has been presented above is one of the classical knowledge representation paradigms in artificial intelligence. There are numerous logical systems, including systems based on fuzzy logic, default logic, modal logic, and temporal logic, to mention only the main ones. These systems all propose frameworks for reasoning techniques. The majority of these logical systems can be specified and implemented in Prolog, using a philosophy similar to that presented in this section.

Chapter 15

An Expert System about Animals

An expert system is a system that possesses knowledge of a limited domain and is capable of effecting reasoning based on this knowledge. It can explain and justify its reasoning about the knowledge. An expert system also often provides a "friendly" user interface. In this chapter, we present a very simple expert system that guesses the name of an animal from the description of certain characteristics. This example is widely discussed in the expert systems literature.

1. Structure of an Expert System

An expert system possesses knowledge about a limited and well-defined domain. This knowledge is often structured according to the type of problem and domain it deals with. The data structure of an expert system is that of a deductive database with an *extensional component* (the facts) and an *intensional component* (the rules).

In answer to questions an expert system is capable of making deductions based on its knowledge. Prolog appears to be the ideal language for the construction of such systems because it already possesses an automatic deduction system. Thus, there is no need to program a deduction mechanism, as is necessary in other languages. Prolog imposes a specific search strategy: top down and left to right, which may not be the ideal one in certain circumstances. However, it is possible to program other strategies.

Expert systems are augmented by communication interfaces. One specialized interface is designed for the input and the updating of data, which are often in considerable quantity. This interface is not dealt with in this chapter. Another interface is dedicated to communication with the user who asks questions. This interface must be friendly and accessible to users without a computing background. It is therefore preferable that the mode of communication be as natural as possible: a simple graphical system or a natural language, English, for example. This interface permits the user to ask questions and at the same time allows the system to reply and to provide explanations.

Another characteristic of an expert system is that it may inform the user of the way in which it has worked out a solution and of which deductions it has made to do so. In a similar way, an expert system may also be capable of informing the user of its abilities so that the user will know what kind of questions can be asked.

An expert system is often capable of reasoning from vague and uncertain information, and may also use default values. As a result, certain deductions will be sorted according to their degree of probability or likelihood, which can be strengthened or weakened. This is the case, for example, in expert systems that aid in medical diagnosis.

An expert system is thus made up of three modules: the data, a system of inferencing called an *inference engine*, and an interface. There is a separation between the data and the inference mechanism: the data depend on the domain of application, whereas the inference mechanism is usable for a vast class of problems. In the data part, knowledge is expressed in a modular fashion, which facilitates the implementation of the expert system. The interface depends partly on the domain, as we shall see in Chapter 17.

The full organization of an expert system can be illustrated as in the following diagram:

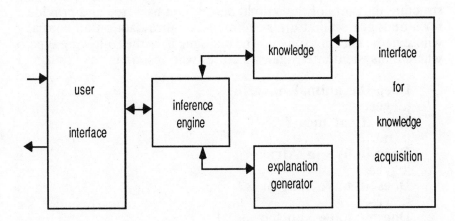

2.   Modeling a Problem

Modeling a domain for an expert system is a long and complex task. It is useful to model the data and the dialogues in conjunction with the user. The data are composed, roughly speaking, of facts and rules of the form

IF *conditions* THEN *result.*

This schema may be completed by adding the probability that the deduction is applicable:

IF *conditions* THEN *result. probability* = **n**.

with **n** less than or equal to 1. It is not always easy to model data according to this type of schema. Moreover, a general method for structuring the data does not exist. In the example that follows, we structure the data as a tree. It is also possible in some cases to use a rewriting system or a grammar. Modeling the data as a tree allows us to go from the more general to the more specific cases, resulting in economy of description, as well as in a certain guarantee of good functionality. It is essential to avoid a "scruffy" representation where the description of the data does not follow a predetermined schema.

Here, the proposed problem is to deduce the names of animals from their biological properties. In more concrete terms, the user wants to know, with the help of the system, the name of an animal he or she is describing.

This example is restricted to a few animals in order to avoid too huge a program. It is, however, easily extendable. We structure the parts of the animal description as a tree and provide for a dialogue so that the system can acquire data on an animal whose name is being sought. The dialogue is of the following type, where the system interrogates the user who responds **yes** or **no**.

Does the animal have fur?
|: yes.
Does it eat meat?
|: no.
Does it live in Africa?
|: yes.
Does it have long legs?
|: yes.
Does it have spotted skin?
|: yes.

The animal is a giraffe.

The following information was deduced from the supplied data:

The animal is a mammal.
This animal lives in Africa.
It has long legs.
It has spotted skin.

The following animals will be considered: bear, sea lion, whale, lion, leopard, giraffe, elephant, heron, gull, ostrich, and penguin.

There are a certain number of characteristics associated with each animal. A sea lion, for example, is a marine mammal that eats fish and has a gray color. A penguin is a sea bird that lives in the water, is black and white, and eats fish. We are thus able to describe numerous animals.

The problems to be solved by an expert system designer are essentially those of selecting all necessary information from the real domain to determine an animal without ambiguity and of organizing and structuring this information.

Organizing the information limits the number of descriptions by grouping together all equivalent pieces of information, taking into account the degree of precision that is needed to process the information. Structuring information allows us to avoid nonlogical or irrelevant questions and also to reach a solution more quickly and in a more reliable way.

In the example presented here, we distinguish between mammals and birds by following the species classification tree. Next, among the mammals, marine animals can be separated from terrestrial animals. Then, carnivores can be distinguished from vegetarians. Among the carnivores, each animal has more specific properties, etc. Note that the structure adopted here is a treelike structure, always with two choices. It is possible to have trees with any number of choices, although they are a bit more difficult to provide a dialogue for.

3. Guessing Names of Animals

We now present the program for this expert system. We first give the knowledge contained in the system. We have attempted to limit the space occupied by these data because in large-scale

applications it is often very large. In our computational model
animals are represented separately as facts. The tree structure of the
properties given above is projected for each animal by means of
numbers referring to the properties it has. Properties are directly
connected to the dialogue interface by the use of these numbers.

Property number 1 is that of a mammal. Its absence signifies
that the animal is not a mammal and, in this expert system, is
therefore a bird. Property number 2 is that of having a carnivorous
diet. Its absence means that the animal has a vegetarian diet.
Property number 3 is that of being able to fly. Etc.

The reader is referred to the interface program to identify the
other properties. Here is the database:

```
animal(sea   lion,[1,2,4,8,18]).
animal(lion,[1,2,5,11]).
animal(leopard,[1,2,5,10,17]).
animal(bear,[1,2,6,8,15,16,17]).
animal(giraffe,[1,5,7,10]).
animal(elephant,[1,5,6,12,13,18]).
animal(heron,[3,7,8,15,18]).
animal(gull,[3,8,14,15,18]).
animal(ostrich,[7,15]).
animal(penguin,[4,8,19]).
```

Here is the dialogue interface:

```
question(1) :- write('Is it an animal that has hair ?'),
nl, !, answer(1).
question(2) :- write('Does this animal eat meat ?'),
nl, !, answer(2).
question(3) :- write('Does this animal fly ?'),
nl, !, answer(3).
question(4) :- write('Does this animal sometimes live in
the water ?'), nl, !, answer(4).
question(5) :- write('Does it live in Africa ?'),
nl, !, answer(5).
question(6) :- write('Does it live in the forest ?'),
nl, !, answer(6).
question(7) :- write('Does it have long legs ?'),
nl, !, answer(7).
question(8) :- write('Does it eat fish ?'),
nl, !, answer(8).
question(9) :- write('Does it have spotted skin ?'),
nl, !, answer(9).
question(10) :- write('Does it have a mane ?'),
```

```
nl, !, answer(10).
question(11) :- write('Does it have tusks ?'),
nl, !, answer(11).
question(12) :- write('Does it have a trunk ?'),
nl, !, answer(12).
question(13) :- write('Does it nest in the rocks ?'),
nl, !, answer(13).
question(14) :- write('Can it be partly white ?'),
nl, !, answer(14).
question(15) :- write('Can it be partly brown ?'),
nl, !, answer(15).
question(16) :- write('Does it climb trees ?'),
nl, !, answer(16).
question(17) :- write('Can it be partly gray ?'),
nl, !, answer(17).
question(18) :- write('Can it be black and white ?'),
nl, !, answer(18).
```

A short program manages the questions and the user's answers. It implicitly traverses the tree of properties.

```
/* Identifying an animal */

identify :- animal(X,Y),
            ask_questions(Y),
            explain(X,Y),
            abolish(discover,2).
identify :- write('Animal unknown.'), nl.
```

```
/* Ask the user questions. */

ask_questions([ ]).
ask_questions([X|Y]) :-  quest(X),
                         ask_questions(Y).

quest(X) :- discover(X,yes), !.
quest(X) :- discover(X,no), !, fail.
quest(X) :- question(X).
```

```
/* Analyze the answer. */

answer(X) :-  read(X),
              insert(discover(X,R)),
              R = yes.
```

The main call is **identify**. It handles the search. It gives explanations to the user through the call **explain**. Finally, to avoid asking the same question several times in case of backtracking, after each question facts of the form **discover(X,Y)** are added, where **X** contains the number of the question and **Y** the answer, **yes** or **no**. At the end of the execution these facts are deleted by a call to **abolish**.

Here is the explanation module invoked either by the program with the call to **explain** or by the user to find out the abilities of the system:

```
explain(X,Y) :- write('The animal is a: '),
    write(X), nl,
    write('This has been deduced from the facts: '),
    nl, explanations(Y).

explanations([]).
explanations([X1|X2]) :- expl(X1), nl,
                            explanations(X2).
```

```
expl(1)    :- write('The animal is a mammal.').
expl(2)    :- write('It is a carnivore.').
expl(3)    :- write('This animal flies.').
expl(4)    :- write('This animal can live in water.').
expl(5)    :- write('This animal lives in Africa.').
expl(6)    :- write('This animal lives in the forest.').
expl(7)    :- write('It has long legs.').
expl(8)    :- write('It eats fish.').
expl(9)    :- write('It has spotted skin.').
expl(10)   :- write('It has a mane.').
expl(11)   :- write('It has tusks.').
expl(12)   :- write('It has a trunk.').
expl(13)   :- write('It nests in the rocks.').
expl(14)   :- write('It can be partly white.').
expl(15)   :- write('It can be partly brown.').
expl(16)   :- write('It climbs trees.').
expl(17)   :- write('It can be gray.').
expl(18)   :- write('It can be black and white.').
```

The reader can augment or modify this expert system. The properties presented here are rough and only partly correspond to reality. However, more detailed and elaborate systems can be built on this model. There are, in fact, very many such systems on the market.

It is also possible to introduce nonclassical logical systems, such as those presented in the preceding chapter. A great deal of literature on expert systems exists; some references are given in the Bibliography. The example presented here is used often because of its simplicity.

4. Toward Actual Expert Systems

Expert systems constitute the most active industrial area of artificial intelligence. Actual expert systems exhibit high levels of complexity and abstraction. They are a test bed particularly well adapted to the evaluation of more abstract research in knowledge representation. The transfer of certain research results to the machine, along with the manipulation of large volumes of complex data, has led in turn to profound improvements in theories of knowledge representation.

Moreover, the characteristics and semantics of Prolog have been studied thoroughly and adapted to suit the characteristics and functionalities of expert systems. This has led to the definition of other languages also belonging to the logic programming paradigm. There are also several expert systems programmed in languages with a very different philosophy, such as object-oriented languages. However, the knowledge in an expert system is usually described in terms of rules, with logic programming languages appearing to be the most suitable.

Chapter 16

Count It Out

The game of "count it out" will permit us to enlarge our understanding of Prolog control mechanisms. We shall see that certain problems are very difficult to express in terms of the somewhat rigid strategy imposed by Prolog. This is particularly the case with the procedure traversal, which is not random but starts with the first clause and continues in the order in which the clauses are written.

The game of "count it out" illustrates this problem in a relatively simple and concise manner. We shall describe the program progressively, imposing constraints on the results.

1. The Basic Game

Let us consider four numbers, **X1**, **X2**, **X3**, and **X4**, and a fifth one **R**. The game "count it out" consists of combining **X1**, **X2**, **X3**, and **X4**, using the standard arithmetic operations (+, -, *, /) to obtain **R** as a result. The numbers **X1**, **X2**, **X3**, and **X4** can be used in any order but may not be used more than once. For example, if we have the four numbers

2, 4, 6, 5

and **R** = 41, a possible combination is

((2 + 4) * 6) + 5).

To simplify the problem, in our first attempt at a solution we assume that the numbers **X1**, **X2**, **X3**, and **X4** must be used in the order in which they are given. We must first find an operator to combine **X1** and **X2**. The result of this operation is then combined with **X3**, and finally, this result is combined with **X4**. Calling the three selected operations **Op1**, **Op2**, and **Op3**, we have

((X1 Op1 X2) Op2 X3) Op3 X4 = R.

The program that resolves this game is invoked with the call

count(X1,X2,X3,X4,R).

and the one that carries out the operation **Op** between **X** and **Y** and stores the result in **Z** is called with

operation(X,Y,Z,Op).

The program **count** is written

```
count(X1,X2,X3,X4,R)  :-
operation(X1,X2,Y1,A),
operation(Y1,X3,Y3,B),
operation(Y3,X4,R,C),
write1([X1,1,A,1,X2,1,B,1,X3,1,C,1,X4,'  =   ',R]).

    operation(X,Y,Z,'+') :- Z is X + Y.
    operation(X,Y,Z,'-') :- Z is X - Y.
    operation(X,Y,Z,'*') :- Z is X * Y.
```

The program **write1** is given in the solution to Exercise 10.1.

To avoid problems with real numbers with the division, we use only addition, subtraction, and multiplication operations.

If we want to allow the combination of **X1** and **X2** and of **X3** and **X4**, and then combine the two results, we get the following formula:

((X1 Op1 X2) Op3 (X3 Op2 X4)).

Our complete program then becomes

```
count(X1,X2,X3,X4,R)  :-
operation(X1,X2,Y1,A),
operation(Y1,X3,Y3,B),
operation(Y3,X4,R,C),  !,
write([X1,1,A,1,X2,1,B,1,X3,1,C,1,X4,'  =   ',R]).

    count(X1,X2,X3,X4,R)  :-
            operation(X1,X2,Y1,A),
            operation(X3,X4,Y2,B),
            operation(Y1,Y2,R,C),
```

```
write1(['(',X1,1,A,1,X2,')',1,C,1,
'(',X3,1,B,1,X4,')   =   ',R]).
```

```
operation(X,Y,Z,'+') :- Z is X + Y.
operation(X,Y,Z,'-') :- Z is X - Y.
operation(X,Y,Z,'*') :- Z is X * Y.
```

2. A More Complex Calculation

The preceding program is somewhat rigid. One cannot, for example, combine **X1** with **X4**, the result with **X2**, and finally, this result with **X3**. It would be interesting to be able to try all the possible combinations of **X1**, **X2**, **X3**, and **X4**, without being constrained by the order in which they are given.

One way to do this is to find all the permutations of the list *[X1,X2,X3,X4]*. This can be done with the program:

perm(L1,L2).

This program gives, through **L2**, all the possible permutations of **L1**:

```
?-  perm([3,7,5,1],L).
```

```
L  =  [3,5,7,1];
L  =  [5,7,1,3];
L  =  [7,1,3,5];
etc.
```

Recall the program given in Chapter 13.

```
perm(L,[H|T]) :-  conc(V,[H|U],L),
                  conc(V,U,W),
                  perm(W,T).
```

```
perm([ ],[ ]).
```

If the result **R** is not found immediately, then different permutations can be tried. The program is written

```
count_it_out(X1,X2,X3,X4,R)  :-
        perm([X1,X2,X3,X4],[Y1,Y2,Y3,Y4]),
        count(Y1,Y2,Y3,Y4,R),  !.
```

```
    count(X1,X2,X3,X4,R)  :-
operation(X1,X2,Y1,A),
operation(Y1,X3,Y3,B),
operation(Y3,X4,R,C),
write1([X1,1,A,1,X2,1,B,1,X3,1,C,1,X4,'  =   ',R]).

    operation(X,Y,Z,'+') :- Z is X + Y.
    operation(X,Y,Z,'-') :- Z is X - Y.
    operation(X,Y,Z,'*') :- Z is X * Y.
```

Cuts were introduced earlier as a way of stopping the program as soon as a solution has been found, in order to limit the execution time of the proof. We only need one definition of **count** since all permutations are tried.

3. Searching for an Approximate Solution

In many cases it is not possible to find a combination of numbers **X1**, **X2**, **X3**, and **X4** that gives **R**. If this happens, we can either abandon the game, saying there is no solution, or attempt to find a solution as close as possible to **R**, with a number either greater or smaller than **R**.

A strategy for finding an approximate value, in the case in which it is not possible to get **R**, is to restart the program with both **R1 = R - 1** and **R1 = R + 1**. A first attempt at such a program is the following, where **approximate** is the main call:

```
approximate(X1,X2,X3,X4,R)  :-
    count_it_out(X1,X2,X3,X4,R),
    !, write('Result found with a total value of: '),
    write(R).
approximate(X1,X2,X3,X4,R)  :-
    R1 is R - 1,
    approximate(X1,X2,X3,X4,R1).
approximate(X1,X2,X3,X4,R)  :-
    R1 is R + 1,
    approximate(X1,X2,X3,X4,R1).
```

In such a program, however, the last clause will never be executed because the second clause must always be executed before it. It will still be possible to find an approximate solution, but it will always be less than **R**. What we would like is to be able to alternate between the second and third procedures. Prolog does not allow this to happen directly. One way to get around this problem is to write a program to manage the alternation of the two clauses, while remembering the attempts that have already taken place.

In the solution presented below, we use two series of facts to memorize actions:

(1) Facts **listenb(R)** memorize the approximate values of **R** that have already been tried, as a way of avoiding useless calculations and, in particular, an infinite number of processes caused by a succession of increments and decrements.

(2) Facts **listattempts(X1,X2,X3,X4,R1)** represent a list of future attempts to find a value of **R1** close to **R**. They are elaborated in clauses 2 and 3 of procedure **count_it_out1**, given below. As soon as these calls have been executed, they are destroyed. These facts can be seen as a list of work still to be done. Here is a program that carries out this approximate search:

```
count_it_out1(X1,X2,X3,X4,R)  :-
            assert(listcount(X1,X2,X3,X4,R)),
            assert(listenb(R)),
            count_it_out2(X1,X2,X3,X4,R).

count_it_out2(X1,X2,X3,X4,Y)  :-
            count_it_out(X1,X2,X3,X4,Y),
            write('Result: '),  write(Y),  !.
count_it_out2(X1,X2,X3,X4,Y)  :-
            Y1 is Y - 1,
            not  listenb(Y1),
            assert(listenb(Y1)),
            assert(listcount(X1,X2,X3,X4,Y1)),
            fail.
count_it_out2(X1,X2,X3,X4,Y)  :-
            Y1 is Y + 1,
            not  listenb(Y1),
            assert(listenb(Y1)),
            assert(listcount(X1,X2,X3,X4,Y1)),
            fail.
count_it_out2(X1,X2,X3,X4,Y)  :-
            listcount(X1,X2,X3,X4,Y1),
            retract(listcount(X1,X2,X3,X4,Y1)),
            count_it_out2(X1,X2,X3,X4,Y1).
```

The main call is **count_it_out1**, which simply creates the facts **listcount(X1,X2,X3,X4,R)**. This fact represents the first task that corresponds to the case in which it is possible to find a combination of values of **X** that are equal to **R**. This is performed by the predicate called **count_it_out2**. The first clause of the procedure **count_it-out2** calls procedure **count_it_out**, given above. If the call succeeds, the approximate value of **R** that satisfies **count_it_out** is displayed, and the program stops because of the cut. The second clause of the procedure **count_it_out2** computes the largest value less than **R** that has not yet been tried. This operation is performed by the following extract from the clause:

Y1 is Y - 1,
not listenb(Y1),

As soon as **Y1** is calculated, if it has not already been used, fact **listenb(Y1)** is added so that **Y1** will not be reconsidered in the future. A work order is added at this time, in the form of fact **listcount**. The third clause performs exactly the same task as the second, with the difference that the smallest value greater than **R** is computed.

After the execution of these two clauses, which both terminate by **fail**, in order to proceed to the fourth, there are two tasks to be carried out. They are stored in **listcount** and contain two approximate values of **R**: one higher and one lower than those that have already been tried. The last clause of the procedure **count_it_out2** activates the tasks until there are no more remaining. A first task is selected by a call to **listcount** and then destroyed, and **count_it_out2** is called one more time. If this call to **count_it_out2** fails (i.e., if the first clause fails, since the two following clauses end with **fail** and thus always fail), then backtracking occurs and another task, stored in the second **listcount** fact, is executed. This will be the task that was formed least recently, because new tasks are inserted following those that already exist.

When the execution of **count_it_out2** (invoked by the fourth procedure) fails, a new task is already waiting. This is done either by the second clause, if the failed call has attempted to find an approximate solution less than **R**, or by the third clause in the opposite case. The last call to procedure **count_it_out2** thus always has another task to execute. The termination of the procedure is determined by the first clause, which suppresses all remaining choices when an answer is found.

Chapter 17

The Automatic Analysis of Natural Language

This chapter is a short introduction to natural language processing in Prolog. Because this area is extremely complex, conceptually as well as technically, we only outline major concepts. Prolog was originally conceived for the translation of simple French sentences into logical formulas. These logical formulas were then transformed into a Prolog program and evaluated on a deductive database. Prolog is thus well adapted to the syntactic analysis of natural or formal languages.

Traditionally, the study of natural languages takes place in many different disciplines. Among these, let us mention the origin of languages, phonology, morphology, syntax, semantics, and pragmatics. In this chapter we concentrate on syntax (describing the structure of sentences) and semantics (extracting the meaning of sentences). For simplicity, each sentence is considered in isolation, apart from any context.

Numerous natural language applications are currently being developed. Most of the time these applications are interfaces to expert systems or deductive databases. The development of these applications, as well as the theoretical work on automatic language processing, has highlighted the extreme complexity of this area.

1. Natural Language and Logic

In the example that we present, the analysis of a natural language sentence is broken down into three stages: syntactic and morphologic analysis, semantic analysis, and the evaluation of the resulting formula on a fact base or the creation of a fact base. This is illustrated in the following diagram:

Natural language sentence

Syntactic analysis (rules + lexicon)

syntax tree

Semantic analysis (interpretation rules + context)

logical formula

Evaluation of the formula (context, evaluation)

Response (a value, yes, no, unknown, creation of data, ...)

It is very interesting to use Prolog to describe this process in its entirety. Prolog can indeed be used to formalize and to implement a syntactic analyzer and the component that calculates the semantic representation of the sentence being analyzed, as well as the formal language of this formal representation. This results in broader conceptual uniformity, as well as in greater ease in manipulating and creating data and, finally, in a simpler implementation.

It should be emphasized that Prolog is only a programming language, even if it exhibits very attractive formal aspects that nicely match some formal aspects of language. Prolog is independent of any linguistic presuppositions.

As will be seen in the succeeding sections, Prolog variables can be used to represent symbolically syntactic and semantic constituents that have not yet been encountered in a sentence being parsed and to formulate constraints on them. This results in greater flexibility and ease in the syntactic and semantic description of sentences.

2. Introduction to Logic Grammar

A *logic grammar* is a context-free grammar in which symbols are augmented by arguments. Furthermore, Prolog predicates can appear at any place in the right-hand side of rules. Arguments that are bound to symbols are used to transfer syntactic and semantic information and to build syntactic and semantic representations. Here, we describe only very simple grammars.

We start with a grammar that analyzes sentences such as *Luke sleeps* and *Edith works*. At a simple logical level, these sentences are represented by **sleep(luke)** and **work(edith)**. The following program carries out the syntactic analysis of the sentence and the construction of its semantic representation in parallel.

```
sentence([P1,P2],RF) :- noun(P1,X),
                        verb(P2,X,RF).

noun(edith,edith).
noun(luke,luke).
verb(sleeps,X,sleep(X)).
verb(works,X,work(X)).
```

This program is composed of a single rule and a lexicon that provides the vocabulary and the semantic representations. Notice the way **X** is bound to a proper noun. To the call

```
?- sentence([edith,works],RF).
```

Prolog responds

RF = work(edith).

We now complete this grammar by adding syntactic and semantic constraints. The simplest way to express constraints in rules is through the use of additional arguments. These constraints range over the values that the variables associated with each of the arguments can take. A rule can only be applied if all constraints are satisfied.

Syntactic constraints are expressed in terms of relationships between words. Among these relationships, those that are concerned with word agreement occupy a prominent place. *Agreement* is understood to be the established convention regarding one or several morphologic components (number, person, etc.) between two or several words in the same sentence. The strongest of these words (e.g., the noun), imposes on one or several other words (e.g., an article or a verb) the necessity of taking the same position as it has, in the different morphologic components.

In each analysis rule, the syntactic features of certain words must be equal to those of other words. To simplify the problem, we retain the following syntactic features:

. For nouns and adjectives, the gender **G** and the number **N** (singular or plural).
. For verbs conjugated in a simple tense, the number **N**. The three singular persons are grouped into the term "singular" (**sing**) and the three plural persons into "plural" (**plu**). Whatever the gender in these conjugated forms, the corresponding argument will be a variable.

The other features are expressed similarly. We now complete the preceding program by adding the constraint that the subject and verb must agree in gender and number. This is not very sensible in English but very crucial in languages like French, Spanish, and case-marked languages like German. It is possible to use the same variable to designate, respectively, the gender and number of the noun and the gender and number of the verb. The program is written:

```
sentence(P1,P3,RF)  :-  noun(P1,P2,G,N,X),
                        verb(P2,P3,G,N,X,RF).

noun([edith|P],P,fem,sing,edith).
noun([john|P],P,masc,sing,john).
verb([thinks|P],P,G,sing,X,think(X)).
verb([think|P],P,G,plu,X,think(X)).
verb([works|P],P,G,sing,X,work(X)).
```

The execution of the call

```
?-  sentence([john,works],[],RF).
```

will have the effect of binding the logical formula **work(john)** to **RF**.

The sentence, represented here as a list of words, is handled in more general fashion.

The rule says that from position **P1** to **P3** there is a sentence, that from **P1** to **P2** there is a noun (which may in some cases be composed of several words), and that from **P2** to **P3** there is a verb:

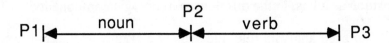

This is expressed in Prolog by binding **P1** to the sentence and **P3** to the empty string: this means that the whole sentence has been parsed. This way of proceeding is more general because no hypothesis is made about the length of the sentence being analyzed. In the first example the representation **[P1,P2]** implies that the sentence does contain exactly two words. This general technique for processing a sentence can be used for any type of syntactic analysis.

Note that in this grammar the variables that represent the gender and the number are the same for the proper noun and the verb. This means that the gender and number of each of these constructions must be the same in this rule for it to be applicable. The reader will easily be able to verify that the call

?- sentence([marie,think],[ ],RF).

will result in a failure.

3. Semantic Constraints

The necessity of employing semantic constraints comes from the fact that a sentence can be syntactically correct and still make no sense. Take, for example, Chomsky's famous sentence:

Colorless green ideas sleep furiously.

It embodies a contradiction because an object cannot at the same time be colorless and colored, in this case green. It also contains what we call *semantic incompatibilities*, since we know that, in a usual context, an abstract entity cannot perform an action or be in a state. In this sentence an idea cannot have a color because an idea is by nature immaterial and also cannot sleep because sleeping is reserved for beings.

From these facts, numerous linguists and psychologists have developed the idea of attributing semantic features to nouns, verbs, etc. Then they established relations that state that the semantic features of a noun, in a given syntactic position (subject, complement, etc.) must verify a certain number of properties in comparison with the semantic features of other words contained in the sentence. These relations are often extremely complex.

The semantic features needed to characterize the words of a subset of English are supposed to be finite and dependent on the chosen application. They are defined by an expert when the lexicon corresponding to the application is specified. For example, *Anne* will have the semantic feature *human* and the word *room* will have the semantic feature *place*.

It must be stressed that a noun cannot accept just any noun complement, and we therefore find it convenient to define the following information for each noun that accepts a noun complement:

(1) The noun's own semantic feature (to simplify, we attribute to a noun a single semantic feature).

(2) A list of the semantic features of nouns that a noun will accept as complements. For example, the word *chair* with semantic feature *physical object* can accept, in some application contexts, noun complements with the semantic feature *object* or *human*.

During the parsing process, when a noun is followed by a noun complement, the parser checks that the semantic type of the noun complement is included in the set of semantic types of acceptable complements for this noun.

Each verb is given the semantic feature of an acceptable subject. It is also associated with a set (eventually empty) of semantic features that characterizes its acceptable complements. In this second semantic relation we consider the verb to be the central element of the proposition. For example, for the verb *to give*, if the subject is of semantic type *human*, then the direct object of the verb must be, for example, of semantic type *material object* and the indirect object must be of semantic type *human* or *animal*.

The application of a rule is thus conditional on the inclusion of the semantic feature associated with each complement in the set of semantic features accepted by the noun or verb.

In the following example, the verification of semantic constraints is done in the same way as the verification of syntactic constraints. We attribute a semantic feature to each noun, and we check, for each verb, the semantic nature of an acceptable subject. We limit ourselves to a single feature. When lists of features are used instead, we must control the inclusion of a feature (e.g., by a call to **member_of**). Other types of semantic agreements are translated into Prolog in the same manner. The previous Prolog program becomes

```
sentence(P1,P3,RF)  :-
              noun(P1,P2,G,N,Sem,X),
              verb(P2,P3,G,N,Sem,X,RF).

noun([marie|P],P,fem,sing,human,marie).
noun([john|P],P,masc,sing,human,john).
noun([fido|P],P,masc,sing,animal,fido).

verb([thinks|P],P,G,sing,human,X,think(X)).
verb([growls|P],P,G,sing,animal,X,growl(X)).
```

The sentence *Marie thinks* is accepted by the grammar, but *John growls* will not be recognized because the subject of the verb *to growl* must be of the semantic type *animal*.

4. Generation of Natural Language

We have already seen several examples in which the same Prolog program can be used to respond to questions with markedly different meanings, depending on which variables, in the call to the program, are free or instantiated. This is, in particular, the case with the program that analyzes natural language sentences presented in the preceding section.

In a call to **sentence(P1,P3,RF)**, if **RF** is bound to a logical formula compatible with those that are formed from formulas contained in the lexicon and if **P3** is an empty list and **P1** is free, Prolog produces a natural language sentence as output. To the call

```
?- sentence(P1,[ ],think(marie)).
```

Prolog responds

P1 = [marie,thinks]

The synthesis of natural language from logical representations is a relatively unexplored area. Major difficulties arise from a linguistic and a stylistic standpoint as well as in the production of a logical formula. Nevertheless, one way that can be profitably explored in this framework is the automatic translation of simple statements.

A very schematic way of translating a sentence from one language into another is to analyze the sentence and transform it into a logical formula. The predicates in the logical formula are then transformed into their equivalents in the target language. This logical representation is transformed into a natural language sentence by using the grammar that describes this language. For example, we might have the following chain for translating English into French:

Mary works -> work(Mary) -> travailler(Marie) -> Marie travaille.

5. Automatic Construction of an Analyzer

In traditional linguistics, a language is often described by a *grammar*. The word grammar, in this context, means a formal system that describes the way in which words are placed to form a correct sentence. Grammars are concerned with the description of the syntax of a language.

The structure of a sentence is described in a top-down fashion. For example, a sentence is composed of a noun phrase (written **np**) and a verb phrase (written **vp**). In the same manner a noun phrase might be composed of an article followed by a noun, or an article followed by a noun followed by a relative clause. A verb phrase might be composed of a verb followed by a noun phrase, or a verb followed by an adverb. This type of description is represented formally by

sentence --> np, vp.
np --> article, noun.
np --> article, noun, relative.
vp --> verb, np.
vp --> verb, adverb.

The symbol **-->** means *is composed of*. The description of the structure of a language is recursive, so that it can describe the numerous "embedded" structures. For example, a relative clause is a sentence embedded into another. The different symbols (**np**, **vp**, **article**, etc.) that appear in the grammar can be augmented with arguments to express constraints in gender, number, and so on.

To avoid using an overly complex notation, we use Prolog's notation for variables. For example, the above grammar becomes

```
sentence --> np(G,N),  vp(G,N).
np(G,N) --> article(G,N),  noun(G,N).
np(G,N) --> article(G,N),  noun(G,N),  relative.
vp(G,N) --> verb(G,N),  np(G,N).
vp(G,N) --> verb(G,N),  adverb.
```

This type of description, frequently used in linguistics, is independent of any automatic processing considerations. It can, however, be transformed very easily into a Prolog program, like those presented in the preceding sections. To do this, we must translate the notation of formal grammars into clausal form and add two arguments to manage the analysis of the words of the sentence. The second task was solved in the preceding sections by the addition of two arguments to each symbol.

Translating the grammar into clausal form is accomplished by replacing the symbol **-->** by **:-** . The symbol **-->** is defined as an operator by the predefined predicate **op**. New clauses are automatically added to the program by a call to **assert**. The addition of variables to control the sentence analysis can be carried out by breaking down each grammar symbol with the operator **=..**, adding two variables, and then reconstructing the symbol with all of its arguments.

We now present a program that performs the transformations explained above. The main call is

transf(R,Clause)

where **R** is a rule and **Clause** the result of the transformation, ready to be inserted into the program by the use of **assert**. The program follows:

```
transf((T --> C),(T3 :- Body)) :- T =.. T1,
                   conc(T1,[X,Y],T2),
                   T3 =.. T2,
                   transf_body(C,Body,X,Y).

transf_body((C,Cs),(C3,Body),X,Y) :- !,
                   C =.. C1,
                   conc(C1,[X,X1],C2),
                   C3 =.. C2,
                   transf_body(Cs,Body,X1,Y).
```

```
transf_body(C,C3,X,Y)  :-  C  =..  C1,
                           conc(C1,[X,Y],C2),
                           C3  =..  C2.
```

Operator **-->** is often predefined in Prolog systems, and the preceding transformation is then performed automatically.

When describing a grammar, it is useful to create a file containing the grammar, which is then transformed directly into a Prolog program. This can be done by declaring the grammar file to be an input file to the transformation program. The result can then be either simply added to the current program (with a call to **grammar**) or deposited in an output file (with a call to **gramoutput**). The program is the following:

```
grammar(F) :-  see(F),
               execute,
               seen.

gramoutput(Finput,Foutput) :- see(Finput),
                              tell(Foutput),
                              execute,
                              seen,
                              told.

execute :-  read(R),
            exec(R).

exec(R) :-  R = end, !.
exec(R) :-  transf(R,Clause),
            assert(Clause),
            execute.
```

Suppose that we call the above program **transformation** and the grammar **gram** (to which we have added the marker **end** after the last line to stop the process). We must then

(1) interpret the two files with the command

[transformation,gram].

(2) invoke the transformation program with the call

?- grammar(gram).

or store the result in an exit file:

?- gramoutput(gram,output-file).

We can now execute the grammar with a call to **sentence**. Using this process, it is possible to construct programs whose goal is to transform a formal grammar or, more generally, a formal language into a Prolog program (when this is theoretically possible). The added arguments may be more complex than those presented here. For example, we might want to have included arguments for the automatic construction of the syntax tree or of a logical formula.

In the same way as for natural language processing, it is possible to construct a program for the analysis of arithmetic expressions and for an interpretor or a compiler for another programming language.

6. A More Complex Logical Formula

The logical formulas constructed by the grammars given in Section 2 are very simple: a single predicate is produced by a sentence and only those constants are manipulated. In this section we propose a more elaborate representation and then show how it can be computed.

The logical representation that we present is known as a three-branched quantified tree. The basic form of this tree representation has determiners as nodes. Three branches leave from each node, introducing, respectively,

(1) a variable, bound to the quantification introduced by the determiner,
(2) the noun phrase (noun and adjectives, along with any relative clauses),
(3) the rest of the sentence.

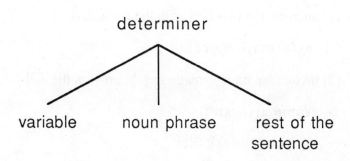

The representation of the subject appears at the top of the tree; this is followed by the representation of the verb complements. The tree terminates on the right with the representation of the verb. For example, the sentence

every country has a capital

is represented by

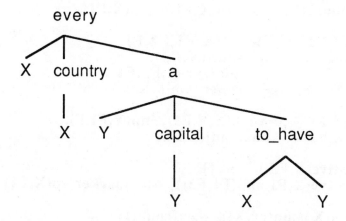

A relative clause is linked to the noun that it modifies by an AND and is included in the nominal subtree.

The car that John owns is fast

is represented as

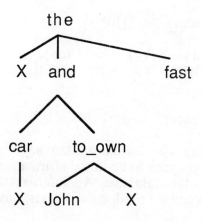

(*John* being a proper noun, it is not subject to quantification and thus appears as a constant of the predicate **to_own**).

The construction of such a representation is quite complex. It is done by describing the tree recursively, forming a new subrepresentation for every determiner in the sentence. The other constituents of the sentence are assembled as arguments of the determiner. Here is the grammar that describes this construction:

```
sentence(F)  -->  np(X,F1,F),vp(X,F1).

np(X,F2,F)  --> det(X,F1,F2,F),
                noun(X,F3),
                relative(X,F3,F1).
np(X,F,F)  -->  proper_noun(X).

vp(X,F)  -->  verb(X,Y,F1),  np(Y,F1,F).
vp(X,F)  -->  aux,  adj(X,F).

relative(X,F,F)  -->  [].
relative(X,F1,and(F1,F2))  -->  marker,vp(X,F2).

noun(X,country(X))  -->  [country].
noun(X,car(X))  -->  [car].
noun(X,capital(X))  -->  [capital].
marker -->  [that].

aux  -->  [is].

adj(X,fast(X))  -->  [fast].

det(X,F1,F2,a(X,F1,F2))  -->  [a].
det(X,F1,F2,the(X,F1,F2))  -->  [the].

proper_noun(john)  -->  [john].

verb(X,Y,to_have(X,Y))  -->  [has].
verb(X,Y,to_own(X,Y))  -->  [owns].
```

7. Toward an Evaluator

Within the framework of a natural language man-machine interface, a sentence analyzed to be in the affirmative leads to the addition of a fact to the database. An interrogative sentence involves an evaluation and the production of a response.

The logical representation introduced above requires some transformations before it can be evaluated in Prolog. In particular, determiners must be appropriately translated, and certain problems involving the scope of quantifiers must be resolved.

The basic method for evaluating a three-branched quantified tree is to transform it into a Prolog program and then to execute this program in order to obtain a response.

Let us consider the example given above:

Every country has a capital.

The determiner *a* translates directly into Prolog, since Prolog questions are implicitly existentially quantified. The determiner *every* is translated by using the equivalence

$$\forall X \ P(X) \Leftrightarrow \neg(\exists X \ \neg P(X))$$

which gives the following formula:

not(country(X), capital(Y), not(to_have(X,Y))).

By reduction of the verb *to have* (another transformation or simplification), we get

not(country(X), not(capital_of(X,Y))).

which becomes, for an interrogative such as

Does every country have a capital?

the following Prolog question:

?- not(country(X), not(capital_of(X,Y))).

However, notice that, if the user has a query of the type

What are the values of X for which P(X)?

it is preferable to use the predicate **setof**:

?- setof(X,P(X),S).

where **S** contains the list of values of **X** that satisfy **P**.

The evaluation phase may be fairly complex. This is not only due to logical problems (e.g., quantification) but also to the expression of the correspondence between logical representations and known concepts in the database. This implies diverse normalizations and transformations that must be treated independently of the analysis of the sentence, since they are not linguistically motivated. Finally, with regard to analysis, it is possible to generate a response in natural language (cf. Section 4) partly by using the logical formula of the query.

Appendix A

Exercise Answers

Here are the answers to the exercises given in the first 10 chapters. We encourage the reader to do each exercise several times until the solution looks trivial to him or her. It is essential that each exercise be well assimilated before the reader goes on to the next one.

Ex. 1.1

(a) A.
(b) B, E, C, G, D.
(c) 3.
(d) parent of B: A;
   children of D: H, I;
   children of C: G, L.

(e)

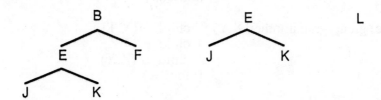

(f) B(E(J,K),F)
   E(J,K)
   L.

Ex. 1.2

(a) give(jack,julie,fido).
(b) brother_of(jack,julie).
(c) courageous(john).

(d) rain.
(e) read(john,hamlet).
(f) author_of(shakespeare,hamlet).
(g) author_of(shakespeare,romeo_and_juliet).
(h) composer_of(mozart,the_magic_flute).

Ex. 2.1

(a) ?- child_of(X,catherine).
(b) ?- blonde(edith).
(c) ?- child_of(paul,john), child_of(martine,john).

Ex. 2.2

(a) catherine, mark.
(b) all the facts of the fact base "taller_than".
(c) john, martine.
(d) Y = john, Z = luke;
     Y = john, Z = marie.

Ex. 3.1

(a) daughter_of(X,Y) :- child_of(X,Y), fem(X).

(b) great_grandfather(X,Y) :- child_of(Y,T),
                               child_of(T,Z),
                               child_of(Z,X),
                               masc(X).

(c) great_grandmother(X,Y) :- child_of(Y,T),
                               child_of(T,Z),
                               child_of(Z,X),
                               fem(X).

Ex. 3.2

(1) know(john,X) :- know(X,john).
(2) know(john,X) :- friend(pierre,X).
(3) friend(me,X) :- friend(Z,X),
                    friend(me,Z).

Ex. 3.3

```
student_of(Student_name,Prof_name) :-
                    course(Prof_name,Course_number),
                    student(Student_name,Course_number).
know(Student,Prof) :- student_of(Student,Prof).
```

Ex. 4.1

(a) S(T1) = f(a(b,c(e,Y)),a(b,c(e,Y))).
(b) S(T2) = g(f(a(b,c(e,Y))),h(a(b,c(e,Y)),3)).
(c) S(T3) = u(a(b,c(e,Y)),f(Y,a(b,c(e,Y)))).

Ex. 4.2

(a) T and U are unifiable: S1(X,a), S2(Y,f(b,c)).

(b) T and U cannot be unified because term names are different (f and g).

(c) T and U cannot be unified because U requires that its two arguments be identical, which is not the case for T.

(d) T and U are unifiable:
                    S1(X,Z)   (variable renaming)
                    S2(T,a)
                    S3(Y,n(W)).

Ex. 6.1

```
larger(X,N) :- X > N, write(X).
larger(X,N) :- N >= X, write(N).
```

Ex. 6.2

```
sum_diff(X,Y,Z) :- X > Y,
                   Z is X + Y.
sum_diff(X,Y,Z) :- Y >= X,
                   Z is X - Y.
```

Ex. 6.3

```
sum_diff1(X,Y,Y) :- X < 0.
sum_diff1(X,Y,Z) :- X >= 0,
                    X > Y,
                    Z is X + Y.
sum_diff1(X,Y,Z) :- X >= 0,
                    Y >= X,
                    Z is X - Y.
```

Ex. 7.1

```
table(10,N) :- R1 is N * 10,
               write('10 times'), write(N),
               write(' = '), write(R1), nl.
table(R,N) :-  R < 10,
               R1 is N * R,
               write(R), write(' times '),
               write(N), write(' = '),
               write(R1), nl,
               R2 is R + 1, table(R2,N).
```

Ex. 7.2

```
ancestor_of(X,Y) :- child_of(Y,X).
ancestor_of(X,Y) :- child_of(Y,Z),
                    ancestor_of(X,Z).
```

If we add the number of generations, we have

```
ancestor_of(X,Y,1) :- child_of(Y,X).
ancestor_of(X,Y,L) :- child_of(Y,Z),
                      ancestor_of(X,Z,L1),
                      L is L1 + 1.
```

Ex. 7.3

```
average :- read(X),
           collect(X,1).

collect(T,N) :- read(X),
                collect1(T,N,X).
collect1(T,N,0) :- M is T / N,
                   write(M).
```

```
collect1(T,N,X) :- not(X = 0),
                   T1 is X + T,
                   N1 is N + 1,
                   collect(T1,N1).
```

Notice that instead of the three last lines, we can also write

collect(X + T, N + 1).

Ex. 8.1

```
diff3(X,Y,Z) :- diff(X,Y),
                diff(Y,Z),
                diff(X,Z).
```

With the following definition for diff:

```
diff(X,X) :- !, fail.
diff(X,Y).
```

diff3 can also be written using negation:

```
diff3(X,Y) :- not(X = Y),
              not(Y = Z),
              not(X = Z).
```


Ex. 8.2

Computing a retail price V from a wholesale price A:

```
retail_price(A,V) :- A =< 100, !,
                     V is (A * 120) / 100.
```

```
retail_price(A,V) :- A > 100, A =< 1000, !,
                     V is (A * 115) / 100.
```

```
retail_price(A,V) :- V is (A * 110) / 100.
```

Ex. 8.3

(a) large_family(X) :- child_of(Y1,X),
                        child_of(Y2,X),
                        child_of(Y3,X),
                        diff3(Y1,Y2,Y3).

diff3 is defined in Ex. 8.1.

(b) friend(john,X) :- person(X),
                       not friend(martine,X).
(c) animal(X) :- not (human(X), object(X), plant(X)).

Ex. 9.1

number_chars([ ],C,0).
number_chars([C|C1],C,N) :- !,
                           number_chars(C1,C,N1),
                           N is N1 + 1.
number_chars([C1|C2],C,N) :- number_chars(C2,C,N).

Selection of a list having exactly three occurrences of the character
'a':

number_chars(L,a,3).

Ex. 9.2

Let the extraction predicate be of the form

extract(L,N,Result).

Then, we have the following definition:

extract(L,0,[ ]).
extract([X1|X2],N,[X1|R1]) :- N1 is N - 1,
                               extract(X2,N1,R1).

Ex. 9.3

extract_last(L,N,R) :- reverse(L,L1),
                        extract(L1,N,R1), reverse(R1,R).

The definition of reverse is given in Chapter 9.

Ex.   9.4

```
subtract([ ],Y,Y).
subtract([X1|X2],Y,Z) :-  withdraw(X1,Y,Y1),
                          subtract(X2,Y1,Z).

withdraw(X,[ ],Y) :-  !, fail.
withdraw(X,[X|Y],Y) :- !.
withdraw(X,[X1|Y],[X1|Z1]) :- withdraw(X,Y,Z1).
```


Ex.   9.5

```
conc_bis([ ],Y,Y).
conc_bis([X|Y],Z,[X|T]) :- not member_of(X,Z), !,
                           conc_bis(Y,Z,T).
conc_bis([X|Y],Z,T) :- conc_bis(Y,Z,T).
```


Ex.   9.6

This program constructs "mutants": "new animals" are created as the result of the coincidence of the end of a word referring to an animal in the fact base and the beginning of another word. We thus obtain, for example, "*caturtle*" from *cat* and *turtle*, which, respectively, ends and begins with the letter *t*. Other examples are "*rabbitch*" from *rabbit* and *bitch* and "*horseal*" from *horse* and *seal*. The letter coincidence is realized via variable B in the two first calls to conc. Notice also that these two first calls are used to decompose lists Y and Z into sublists.

Ex.   10.1

```
write1([X|Y]) :-  integer(X), !,
                  tab(X), write1(Y).
write1([X|Y]) :-  write(X),
                  write1(Y).
```

Appendix B

Main Predefined Predicates

abolish(C,N)
Deletes definition C with arity N.

abort
Stops execution of the current call.

arg(N,T,A)
The nth argument of the term T is A.

assert(C)
Asserts clause C at the end of the already existing definition that C complements.

asserta(C)
Asserts clause C at the beginning of the already existing definition that C complements.

atom(T)
Term T is an atom.

atomic(T)
T is an atom or an integer.

bagof(X,P,S)
S is the set of X satisfying P. An identical value may appear several times in S.

close(F)
Closes file F.

display(T)
Prints T.

fail
Provokes an immediate backtrack.

functor(T,F,A)
F is the functor of term T with arity A.

get(C)
Reads the next nonblank character and binds C to it.

get0(C)
Reads the next character and binds C to it.

halt
Stops Prolog system.

integer(T)
Term T is an integer.

A is B
A is bound to the result of the arithmetic expression B.

listing
Lists the current program.

listing(C)
Lists the current definition of C.

nl
Begins a new line before printing.

notrace
Stops tracing.

novar(T)
Term T is not a variable.

number(N)
N is a number.

op(P,T,A)
Defines operator A with priority P and type T.

put(C)
Prints character C.

read(T)
Reads a string of characters and binds it to T.

retract(C)
Deletes the first clause C encountered in the current program.

save(F)
Saves the current program in file F.

see(F)
F is the new input file.

seen
Closes the current input file. The screen is the new input file.

setof(X,P,S)
S is the set of X satisfying P. Duplicates are deleted.

sort(L,L1)
L1 is the sorted list L.

statistics
Gives statistics on executions.

tab(E)
Prints E spaces.

tell(F)
F is the new current output file.

told
Closes the current output file.

trace
Starts tracing.

var(T)
T is an unbound variable.

write(X)
Writes X.

!
Suppresses the remaining choices (cut).

not P
Is true if P cannot be proved.

X < Y
X is smaller than Y.

X =< Y
X is smaller than or equal to Y.

X > Y
X is greater than Y.

X >= Y
X is greater than or equal to Y.

X = Y
X matches Y.

X == Y
X and Y are strictly identical.

X =.. Y
Y is the decomposition (a list) of term X. This predicate also permits the construction of a term X from a list Y.

[X|Y]
List notation: X is the head and Y is the tail of the list.

Bibliography

Here are some books that will permit the reader to deepen his or her understanding of Prolog. The absence from this list of some books on Prolog should not be interpreted as an implicit judgment on their value.

BRATKO I. [1986]. Prolog Programming for Artificial Intelligence. Addison-Wesley.

CLARK K., TARNLUND S.A. (Eds.) [1982]. Logic Programming. Academic Press.

CLOCKSIN W.F., MELLISH C.S. [1984]. Programming in Prolog. Springer-Verlag, 2nd edition.

COELHO H., COTTA J.C. [1988]. Prolog by Example. Springer-Verlag.

GALLAIRE H., MINKER J. [1978]. Logic and Databases. Plenum Press.

KOWALSKI R. [1979]. Logic for Problem Solving. North Holland.

LLOYD J. [1987]. Foundations of Logic Programming. Springer-Verlag, 2nd edition.

PEREIRA F., SHEIBER S. [1986]. Prolog for Natural Language Analysis. CSCI lecture notes, Chicago University Press.

STERLING L., SHAPIRO E. [1986]. The Art of Prolog. MIT Press.

Index

Terms in italics refer either to major Prolog programs given in the book and used in several examples or to predefined Prolog procedures. Page numbers refer to the definition of the terms mentioned and not to all their occurrences.